ESCAPE THE WOLF
A Security Handbook for Traveling Professionals

Clinton Emerson

First published by Dog Ear Publishing
4011 Vincennes Rd
Indianapolis, IN 46268
www.dogearpublishing.net

ISBN: 978-1-5985-8967-2

This book is printed on acid-free paper.

Printed in the United States of America

About the author

Clinton Emerson is a retired 20-year Navy SEAL, who served with the National Security Agency (NSA) and the elite DEVGRU, entrepreneur and best-selling author. Escape the Wolf, the company Emerson founded, is a risk mitigation company that provides preemptive, holistic security solutions for global companies and government agencies focused on crisis management policy, planning and workforce education. His experience in risk mitigation and crisis management is highly sought after in today's crisis-torn world. Mr. Emerson is a regular Fox Business *Firewall* contributor and author of *Escape the Wolf* and the new best-seller *100 Deadly Skills*.

Table of Contents

Preface

Why do some travelers seem to invite crime?

What steps can you take to make yourself less vulnerable?

How can you minimize exposure to illness, natural disasters and other threats when traveling?

This book will show you how to avoid being a "walking target" and provides a holistic approach to avoiding and minimizing threats while traveling.

Awareness is the key.

Remember how uneasy you felt the first time you visited an unfamiliar place? Listen to that sense of unease, as it may very well be warranted.

The lessons shared in this book can help put you at ease and keep you safe, whether you are traveling around the globe or around the corner. Some of the examples in this book may appear to be on the extreme side. In reality, they could easily happen to any traveler with the bad luck to stumble upon on a nefarious scheme. I speak from experience. As you'll see, each and every one of these scenarios have happened to me.

The business of travel security generally deals with **low-probability** occurrences. Does that mean you should ignore the threats? After all, you're more likely to get in a car accident near your home than to have something happen when traveling abroad. The problem with that line of thinking is that travel security is a **high-risk** issue. If something *does* happen while you are traveling internationally, the stakes are high, and you have fewer resources to draw upon.

What if your wallet gets lifted? What if you are the victim of a carjacking or hotel intrusion? What if you become ill or are in the aftermath of a hurricane or earthquake? What if you are thrown in jail in a foreign country because of a misunderstanding? What if you are kidnapped? Or become the victim of a terrorist operation? Each of these scenarios has a varying degree of likeliness. But an understanding of travel security is like a life insurance policy. Why not proceed with a good, solid plan?

Escape the Wolf's goal is to prepare the global traveler to cope with the unexpected. I started this book because of my observations and interactions with U.S. government employees. It amazed me that so much money was being spent in terms of equipment, education and preparation for international travel. Yet one important thing was missing from these employees' suitcases—basic awareness training.

Awareness training is something that I, and other folks who travel to high-risk areas during the course of our daily jobs, have drawn upon to avoid and minimize trouble.

When I began sharing the insights of awareness training with these travelers, they responded so positively that I decided to write this book.

What they and others have found is that basic awareness training is useful not only as a risk mitigation tool but also as a valuable form of cultural currency. Because awareness training can make it possible for travelers to forge successful relationships with individuals in the local culture, it has the potential to make any business traveler's stay more pleasant and smooth.

Introduction:

Of Sheep, Wolves and Sheepdogs –
Which One Are YOU?

A dark and foreboding creature found throughout the ages in fairy tales from "Little Red Riding Hood" to Russia's "Peter and the Wolf," the wolf is a near-universal symbol for a predator. In these and other cautionary tales, the dangers that lurk just beyond the safety of the familiar village are embodied in the form of the wild and restless animal.

Escape the Wolf takes its title from this symbol, but more specifically from the imagery evoked by Lt. Col. Dave Grossman, who has spoken so eloquently about the root causes of the current wave of violent crime that threatens the world. A former West Point psychology professor, professor of military science and Army Ranger, Grossman is one of the world's foremost experts in the field of human aggression and the roots of violence and violent crime. In *On Combat: The Psychology and Physiology of Deadly Conflict, In War and In Peace,* he paints a vivid picture of awareness and gives us language that helps us define the threats average citizens face:

> "Most of the people in our society are sheep. They are kind, gentle, productive creatures who can only hurt one another by accident. This is true. Remember, the murder rate is six per 100,000 per year, and the aggravated assault rate is four per 1,000 per year. What this means is that the vast majority of Americans are not inclined to hurt one another. Some estimates say that two million Americans are victims of violent crimes every year, a tragic, staggering number, perhaps an all-time record rate of violent crime. But there are almost 300 million Americans, which means that the odds of being a victim of violent crime is considerably less than one in a hundred on any given year. Furthermore, since many violent crimes are committed by repeat offenders, the actual number of violent citizens is considerably less than two million.

> "Thus there is a paradox, and we must grasp both ends of the situation: We may well be in the most violent times in history, but violence is still remarkably rare. This is because most citizens are

kind, decent people who are not capable of hurting each other, except by accident or under extreme provocation. They are sheep.

"I mean nothing negative by calling them sheep. To me it is like the pretty, blue robin's egg. Inside it is soft and gooey but someday it will grow into something wonderful. But the egg cannot survive without its hard blue shell. Police officers, soldiers, and other warriors are like that shell, and someday the civilization they protect will grow into something wonderful. For now, though, they need warriors to protect them from the predators.

"These predators are 'the wolves,' and the wolves feed on the sheep without mercy. Do you believe there are wolves out there who will feed on the flock without mercy? You better believe it. There are evil men in this world and they are capable of evil deeds. The moment you forget that or pretend it is not so, you become a sheep. There is no safety in denial.

"The warriors are 'sheepdogs'…and I'm a sheepdog. I live to protect the flock and confront the wolf. If you have no capacity for violence then you are a healthy productive citizen, a sheep. If you have a capacity for violence and no empathy for your fellow citizens, then you have defined an aggressive sociopath, a wolf. But what if you have a capacity for violence, and a deep love for your fellow citizens? What do you have then? A sheepdog, a warrior, someone who is walking the hero's path. Someone who can walk into the heart of darkness, into the universal human phobia, and walk out unscathed."

For the purposes of this book, let's extend the definitions of the sheep, sheepdog, and wolf as they relate to awareness. Sheep, according to LTC Grossman, are people who appear to be weak. They go about their business with their heads down and do not really worry about their surroundings. Sheep have a predictable daily schedule or routine and never step outside their comfort zone. This means that sheep are easily targeted by wolves because of their submissive, hunched-over posture and complete lack of attention, especially to the environment around them. Another vocabulary note: When sheep die at the fangs of a wolf, they are called victims.

Grossman's sheepdog is a whole different animal. He is locked in at all times. His ears are up, his nose sensitive to the winds. Sheepdogs present themselves as dominant and intimidating to better manage the flock, but also to ward off potential threats. They are smart, athletic and motivated leaders. A sheepdog will engage in battle with the proper amount of force to neutralize the enemy, and to kill if necessary. Sheepdogs are our police force and our military. When sheepdogs die at the fangs of a wolf, they are called heroes.

Using the Grossman definition, the evil wolf represents all kinds of possible threats. Wolves are health threats, environmental threats, raids or attacks, technological threats, and of course, criminals and terrorists. Wolves run in packs. Where there is one, there are many. The minute you engage just one, you will find yourself surrounded. When wolves die at the fangs of a sheepdog, they are just dead bad guys.

I invite you to embrace Grossman's mindset and to keep my definitions of the sheep, sheepdog, and wolf in mind. These terms will be helpful shorthand as we explore the concept of awareness more fully.

Chapter 1

The Total Awareness System

Africa. I'm up early, before the sun. The day starts out like every other in my three-month assignment in the city. To get a head start on work, I plan to get in early. I turn the key to the rental SUV. The engine springs to life, breaking the deathly stillness. The only other sound is the low hum of a rudimentary power line in my temporary housing. I pull out of the driveway, breathe in the cool, dry air, and survey the narrow dirt road ahead. My headlights illuminate the sultry blackness.

The first three miles of my trip into the city never vary. No choice—there aren't any turn-offs or side streets, just this single, bumpy lane. Even without traffic, it's slow going, splashing through rain-filled pot-holes. Less than a mile into this familiar trek, I notice a man with his back to me, sitting on a motorcycle with no lights on, parked in a residential driveway along the lane. It's a little odd, but nothing out of the ordinary. Africans tend to be up at all times of night. Second mile into my trip, a car with its hood up is smack in the roadway. A second car sits behind it. I'm about 500 yards away, going downhill. At that moment, a single headlight bounces off my rear view mirror. It's the motorcycle. The second car pulls next to the car with the raised hood. Now the entire road is blocked.

Decision time. Should I stop here? There is someone behind me and in front of me. Others could be lurking in the tree line to my right and left. Do I throw my car into reverse and head back the way I came, recognizing that my escape options are limited? Or, should I keep the momentum going and go for broke?

Practical Example – What would YOU do?

Think this scenario could only be found in a movie? Think again. This real-life scenario happened to me, the author.

The setup you just read could be the beginning of a carjacking, a kidnapping, or something far worse. It might take place in Africa, South America or any other continent. Global travelers face many dangers. Recognizing and preparing for them makes all the difference.

In the following chapters, we'll explore Escape the Wolf's Total Awarenessä System. This proven approach prepares travelers for the unexpected, whether it's random crimes like pick pocketing and carjacking, or more serious issues like kidnapping.

In this case, I chose to hit the gas and drove toward the two cars, which now had their high-beam headlights trained on me. At the last moment, I cut left and drove up a 45-degree embankment, missing the other vehicle by inches and knocking off my mirror in the process. I took the option they didn't expect—coming right at them. As a result, I caught them off guard. Thanks to extensive preparation, I made the right decision without having to go through lengthy and potentially dangerous deliberations. As a result, I was able to continue on my merry way.

Why were my assailants counting on me to do the expected? What did I do to change the game? What can you do?

Most Americans would stop to help. We stop to let oncoming traffic pass. At the very least, most Americans would hesitate long enough for the bad guys' real plan to unfold. But that's not the way it has to go down.

"The real voyage of discovery consists not in seeking new landscapes but in having new eyes." —Marcel Proust

Building the Skill of Awareness

One survival threat we seldom consider: modernity. Our basic human survival skills are being lost, replaced by technology and obscured by the busyness of everyday life. In general, people do not pay attention to their surroundings. When crisis strikes, they mentally stall and fall victim to preventable demise. People don't pull their heads out of their smartphones and tablets long enough to notice the clues that signal danger. We are losing our ability to be aware.

Some equate awareness to a sixth sense. Men call it instinct. Women call it intuition. Either way, it is one important way that we detect threats. Instinct is emotionally, subconsciously powered and very rarely interpreted by the brain. The "spidey senses" of some individuals seem to be evolved at higher levels, but can such awareness be taught?

As part of the research for this book, I conducted a brief survey of individuals in different occupations where awareness is instrumental to successful outcomes. The survey included fighter pilots, law enforcement SWAT officers, FBI agents, CIA clandestine operatives, special operation military operators, surgeons and others. I asked, "Do you believe some people are born with a heightened sense of awareness?" The overwhelming answer was yes.

The next question in the survey was "Do you believe awareness can be taught?" Again, the overwhelming answer was "Yes." These experienced, educated professionals agreed that some people are born with a heightened sense of awareness, but that awareness can be taught. Still, awareness is contextually based.

Even if you have great instincts, how good are those instincts going to be in an unfamiliar environment? When traveling, your instincts are hypercharged, firing off false alerts when you are first exposed to foreign surroundings.

Remember that Halloween when you dressed as your favorite superhero and waited in line at the season's first haunted house? You stood listening to the screams and let the anticipation flow. You entered, watching at every corner, listening to every sound, and all the while trying so hard not to be frightened. No matter how hard you tried, you still got scared to death. Every time you thought something would happen—nothing. But the rest of the time, you jumped out of your skin. Stepping foot into another country can be the same. Your instincts tell you one thing, but the results are entirely different. Eventually, the false alerts desensitize your instincts. That can make you vulnerable to surprise or attack. The Total Awareness system will keep your guard up when your natural defense systems are down.

One person who was surveyed made an interesting point. He agreed that awareness skills could be taught, but questioned whether *anyone* could make the right decisions, under stress, after potentially dangerous clues are recognized. Interesting point.

How many times have you made the wrong decision in a critical or dramatic situation? When critiquing the information post-event, you've beaten your head against the wall, called yourself an idiot, and said, "I knew that was going to happen, but did nothing!" The answer is simple. You saw all the clues, did nothing, and you were an idiot.

Connecting the dots and reacting in an effective manner takes education, experience and practice. To be successful, you have to recognize and analyze available clues and react swiftly. To constantly be aware of surroundings and make effective decisions based on clues and cues requires a change of lifestyle. The Total Awareness approach is a lifestyle. Like any skill, it takes practice. You need to do it all the time to be good at it. If it is not a lifestyle, failure increases exponentially, especially in dangerous environments.

Awareness is a weapon. If used properly, it can conceal your movements, ward off potential threats, prevent attacks, and ultimately, save your life and the lives of others. Awareness is free. It never runs out and is issued to each and every person who walks the earth. Harnessing the power of awareness can be difficult and tiring. With practice, however, awareness can become as natural as walking.

In this book, I will define the Total Awareness system and its components, showing you how to use this awareness to minimize and avoid threats while traveling. I'll give you tools and processes that will help you make good decisions without hesitation. First, you must understand that the Total Awareness system is more than just observation and instinct. It's a research and assessment tool to be used before traveling or entering unknown territory.

The Total Awareness™ System

The Total Awareness (TA) System is a risk assessment system that manages and reduces risks—or threat vulnerabilities—for the global traveler. The structured Total Awareness approach can be used by anyone but is designed for the professional traveler—the diplomat, government employee, journalist or businessperson.

Third Party Awareness | Personal Awareness | Cultural Awareness | Situational Awareness

Components of the Total Awareness System

The Total Awareness system can be broken down into a set of components that, taken together, create a complete awareness profile. These components include:

- **Situational Awareness (SA)**, *a conscious and constant focus on the environment* that seeks to detect, validate and confirm threats. Your ability to detect potential threats can be a result of both instinct and observation. This chapter will discuss situational awareness in detail.

- **Personal Awareness (PA)**, *the image and demeanor you project.* Your demeanor can help you blend into a specific culture, reduce your threat exposure and reduce your visibility to others—or it can increase your vulnerability to risk. Honing your Personal Awareness will give you the ability to assess and manage specific character traits that could potentially make you stand out from the culture where you will be traveling. Chapter 3 will discuss Personal Awareness in detail.

- **Cultural Awareness (CA)**, *the assessment and understanding of the culture in a specific geographic location.* This awareness component covers areas such as cultural-specific social protocol, etiquette, mannerisms and gestures. By combining Cultural and Personal Awareness, you will gain the ability to blend into the local culture and avoid standing out as a potential target. Chapter 4 will discuss Cultural Awareness in detail.

- **Third-Party Awareness (3PA),** *the general public's perception of you and your actions.* In a nutshell, when you feel like everyone is staring at you, they probably are. Third-Party Awareness extends to groups like citizens, law enforcement, criminals, and even terrorists residing in the host country. Reducing Third-Party Awareness requires you to blend into the environment using Personal Awareness (managing the way your image and demeanor is projected within a cultural setting) and Situational Awareness skill sets. Chapter 5 will discuss 3PA in detail.

- **THREAT®** *is a risk-assessment tool* and an acronym that stands for Technical, Health, Raid, Environmental, Agency, and Terror threats in a specific geographic location. An educated global traveler will research and assess these threats before any international trip. By taking a holistic view of threats, you can prepare your senses, adjust your Situational and Personal Awareness, and decrease your vulnerabilities. Chapter 6 will discuss THREATs in detail.

Even when you are effectively practicing the Total Awareness system— fully locked in, absorbing and processing the information all around you like Jason Bourne of *The Bourne Identity*—you can still be caught off-guard by forces beyond your control. But even when taken by surprise, your reaction time and decision-making process will be better primed for effective action. Understanding the components of awareness can help you take control of forces normally *out* of your control.

To implement the Total Awareness system, you will need to properly assess and research a specific destination, prepare your senses and adapt your Personal Awareness traits. Once you are in an environment, you must begin to identify third parties and potential threats in an orderly fashion in a limited amount of time. To do this, you will follow a mental checklist (covered in detail in the following pages) that will enable you to manage the information you take in and make decisions based on instinct and observation.

Taking these steps will ultimately enable you to escape the wolf.

Situational Awareness

Situational awareness enables you to focus on what is happening all around you. You take in all the information in the environment, recognizing how your own actions and the actions of others may influence the outcome.

Think about the difference between the experience of learning to drive a car and the way you now have internalized the process. You no longer hit the brake every time you see another car. You've learned to distinguish between false alarms and real threats, like the teenager who barrels through a red light. Eventually, the process for detecting travel security and safety threats will become the same. You will start to internalize this process, which keeps instinctively charged alerts in check with observed actions within the environment. Situational Awareness does just that and more.

Types of Environments

As we start to learn about Situational Awareness, we must first define and understand the environment. The amount of control the local government has over crime, corruption and other potential threats to the community and everyone in it—including you—is an important consideration in your planning and preparation. Your preparations will differ in countries where the local government isn't strong, say in a country like Mexico, from the planning you would undertake when visiting a country where the local government is fairly strong, like the United Kingdom.

The globe can be divided into three kinds of environments, via U.S. government terminology used to assess international travel threats:

> ***Permissive environment*** - An area that is completely controlled by the government. Its citizens support the government. Most im-

portantly, the host government and its citizens support the United States. Utopia, if you will, where everyone lives in harmony. Not sure a fully permissive environment truly exists—Canada maybe?

Semi-permissive environment - A government with questionable control. The citizens may or may not support the government. Corruption is usually the wolf in these locations. The government and citizens may or may not support the United States. Country example: Philippines. Most of the world is semi-permissive.

Non-permissive environment – An area where little or no government exists, sometimes called a denied area. Control is induced through the hostile actions of non-government forces. Support of the United States or its citizens is minimal. Country examples: Somalia.

Note that though I defined each environment as an area, using countries as examples, all three environments can exist within one country, province or city. Two of the three exist in the United States. Permissive is not one of them.

You will want to research the area that you will be visiting. What sort of environment(s) will you encounter?

Identifying Real Threats from False Ones

As you'll recall, **Situational Awareness (SA)** is the practice of focusing consciously and constantly on the environment around you to detect, validate and confirm threats. How do you screen out false alarms from real threats? The best way is through an approach that I call the **Modes of Awareness™ (MOA)** cycle. Just like the environment, Situational Awareness can be broken into a mental cycle (MOA), which you rotate through as threats present themselves.

OODA Loop

It's hard to make good decisions when you are stressed and time crunched. As a result, I've incorporated a tactical decision-making process called the OODA loop (**O**bservation, **O**rientation, **D**ecision, and **A**ction) within the Modes of Awareness cycle.

Found in dozens of military and business strategy books, the OODA loop is a dynamic tool for tactical decision-making developed by John

Boyd, a U.S. Air Force fighter pilot. It was the approach that helped him win a standing bet to all newcomers as a pilot. Starting from a disadvantage in flight, he could lock on a missile within 40 seconds—or he'd pay 40 dollars, a fair chunk of change during his time. According to legend, he never lost, in large part because of the decision-making process that earned him the nickname "Forty Second" Boyd.

Boyd hypothesized that all intelligent organisms and organizations undergo a continuous cycle of interaction with their environment. He described four interrelated and overlapping processes through which an organism continuously cycles in a loop he believed to be critical to survival. The components of the OODA loop are:

- **Observation**, the collection of information or data by means of the senses.

- **Orientation**, the analysis and computation of collected information and data to form a real-time mental perspective.

- **Decision**, the course of action to be taken based on your current perspective.

- **Action**, the physical play-out of the decision.

Practical Travel Example

Let's take a practical travel example. Say you are on business in a semi-permissive environment in the city of New Delhi in India. Your hotel is only a few blocks from the company you are going to meet with. Since you are running late, you decide to walk and skip the traffic jams. There is a short-cut, the same alley that your dinner companion from the night before used. It will save you precious time. The alley is not well lit, and you think you see some movement. Should you go in, or take the longer way across an open square? You only have a few minutes to make a quick decision. You can take care of yourself in most instances. But is this a case where you want to gamble?

Using Situational Awareness, your research should have begun at home. You would have learned that petty crime is common in India, as is the theft of U.S. passports, especially in major tourist areas. Some westerners, especially U.S. citizens, have been the victims of violent attacks, especially when they are alone. You should use the same common sense that you would when at home. Would you venture into an alley alone in New York City? Be especially cautious in known target areas for crime, like train stations, poorly lit areas, alleys, market sites and crowded areas.

Using the OODA loop, you would **observe** by surveying the alley and the shadowy movement. Then you would **orient** by analyzing the data, both the research you've done before your trip and the visual survey you've just completed. You would **decide**, which in this case would be to choose the alternative of the safer, more open route. And, you would complete the loop by **acting**, actually walking across the square and avoiding the alley and the potential robber.

Boyd's loop is a commonsense approach. It's also an elegant framework for creating a competitive advantage. Not only can you observe, orient, decide and act, but you can also get inside the head of your opponent's OODA loop. It's what basketball players do when they fake a move on the court. Imagine operating "inside" the wolf's OODA loop, so you can out think and out maneuver threats.

The real takeaway is the cycle or loop itself. Each stage of the loop relates to the other, leading to a speedy tactical decision. I have integrated this loop into each of the Modes of Awareness cycle to eliminate indecisiveness in times of crisis. Using the OODA loop to guide your transitions from mode to mode will force observation, orientation, and decision prior to acting. The loop prevents action without planning—and as everyone knows, the difference between an emergency and chaos is having a plan.

If you decide to read some of Boyd's theories, be warned that he did a great job of making the OODA loop the equivalent to rocket science. In my opinion, simple is good, particularly when it comes to survival. The less there is to remember, the better.

The Modes of Awareness Cycle

The Modes of Awareness cycle is a continuum of alertness, which can be divided into three stages—*Alert, Pre-Crisis*, and *Crisis*. You can shift from mode to mode by second, minute, hour or day, depending on the perceived threat and the environment around you.

Often in a wolf-rich environment, your senses of feeling, sight, smell and sound are your best assets. The pressure of a hand against your wallet, the smell of smoke, the sight of a crowd, or the sound of a gunshot should all trigger responses and cause you to adjust your awareness as you move through the appropriate phases of the Modes of Awareness cycle. During this process, you will be setting invisible thresholds that act as lines or trip-wires. If breached or crossed, these thresholds will initiate your actions. An action could be as simple as transitioning from mode to mode, or as dynamic as acting out a decision to fight or escape the potential threat.

Here are the Modes of Awareness — Alert, Pre-Crisis, and Crisis — defined:

Alert Mode

Potential Time in Mode: *Hours, Days, Months*

Alert Mode – Alert Mode is the constant observation of the environment, a perpetual scan for potential threats. You should be in Alert Mode the majority of the time you are traveling. Time in Alert Mode may last days, weeks, or months. Transition from Alert to Pre-Crisis Mode is triggered by the recognition of potential threats. To avoid freezing or stalled decisions, set invisible thresholds and use the OODA loop process to manage your reactions.

• You are in alert or preparatory phase. You are always mentally preparing to move to the next level. Within Alert, you are identifying, positioning and acting based on POTENTIAL threats.

   • *Observation* – You are feeling, looking, listening and smelling your environment.

   • *Orientation* – You are mentally changing your position based on the information being collected and processed from potential threats.

   • *Decision* – You are constantly making decisions to mitigate any potential threats.

   • *Action* – You are acting on the decisions to maintain the greatest advantage over perceived potential threats. You are deliberately trying to confirm potential threats.

Pre-Crisis Mode

Potential Time in Mode: *Minutes, Hours*

Pre-Crisis Mode – Pre-Crisis Mode is the constant observation of identified potential threats. Time in Pre-Crisis Mode may last hours or days. This mode allows a person to determine courses of action and designates an invisible threshold that activates Crisis Mode. The decisions made in this mode allow you to be in the best position should the Crisis Mode become necessary. If the threat breaches the invisible threshold, then you initiate Crisis Mode.

- In Pre-Crisis, you are identifying, positioning and acting based on CONFIRMED threat(s).

  - *Observation* – You feel, see, hear or smell the confirmed threat(s).

  - *Orientation* – You are physically and mentally changing your position to gain the greatest advantage over the confirmed threat(s).

  - *Decision* – You are constantly reevaluating the environment, developing courses of action to increase your odds of mitigation and escape from the confirmed threat(s).

  - *Action* – You are setting invisible thresholds that will initiate Crisis Mode if breached by the threat(s). You are arranging the situation to prepare for Crisis Mode.

Crisis Mode

Potential Time in Mode: *Seconds, Minutes*

Crisis Mode – Crisis Mode is when you take tactical act against the threat. At this stage, your goal is to elude, escape or dominate the threat so you can quickly and successful transition back to Pre-Crisis Mode. It's no time for decision-making, which should have been completed in Pre-Crisis Mode. Crisis Mode is triggered by the breach of the invisible threshold you have set. Crisis Mode may last seconds or minutes. Transitioning back to Pre-Crisis Mode should occur sooner rather than later. Prolonged exposure to the threat may decrease survivability.

- You are actively ENGAGED with the threat(s). In full-on crisis mode, you are attacking, defending yourself against, or escaping the threat(s). You are identifying, positioning, and acting against the threat(s) to return to Pre-Crisis Mode as quickly as possible.

  - *Observation* – You are feeling, looking, listening and smelling for a Pre-Crisis environment.

  - *Orientation* – You are physically and mentally changing your position based on the information being processed in the Crisis Mode.

  - *Decision* – You are constantly making decisions that will mitigate or eliminate the threat(s).

  - *Action* – You are acting out the decisions that will enable you to defeat the threat, survive and return to Pre-Crisis Mode.

Practical Travel Example

Let's use another real-life travel example to illustrate how the MOA cycle works. I was once assigned to train another country's secret organization on how to conduct surveillance operations. Surveillance is one of those skills that can't be taught solely in a classroom, and unfortunately, I was in an environment where much of the population disliked Westerners. But my assignment meant I had to conduct training among the people, moving around in a hostile community without the population knowing that surveillance training was taking place.

I teach surveillance based on the systematic, team-based static and mobile observation of a target. Fundamentally, there are only two phases of any surveillance, the "pick up" and the "follow." The "pick up" is the point at which the surveillance team sets up on the target and waits for the target to move. The "follow" is the discreet trail behind or ahead of the target during movement. That may sound simple, but surveillance is very difficult to master, hampered by elements such as lack of area knowledge, poor communication equipment, personnel constraints, and surprise obstacles that slow or prevent a team from maintaining eyes on its target.

After some classroom time teaching the basics, it was time to get out and try it. I decided to be the target and let the team follow me for an hour or so, after which I planned for us to head back to the classroom to debrief. I had already selected a walking route, with the goal of having the team keep me under observation without being detected by me, the target. If the technique is done correctly, I shouldn't know that I'm being followed, because each member of the team will rotate through different positions and never allow me to see the same face twice. New teams usually fail miserably at this for days and even weeks.

So there I am, walking through a town where the local population is less than fond of Westerners, trying to keep track of my team to accurately debrief them. Of course, I am very ALERT, on the lookout for potential threats as I scanned the crowds, observing and orientating myself to people and faces to distinguish students from real threats.

Ahead, I notice two young men walking toward me on the same side of the street. From a distance, their facial expressions say, "I hate you." I recognize that they are not my students. In Alert Mode, I observe them and decide that crossing the street and continuing in the same direction of travel is the best option. I decide to make the street my invisible threshold, which will trigger Pre-Crisis Mode. If they cross as well, then I will go into Pre-Crisis Mode (confirming the threat). So I nonchalantly cross the street, as if that's what I planned, doing so without giving the two young men any obvious attention.

Now I had plenty of space between them and me. I was already thinking about Pre-Crisis Mode and what I was doing next if they breached the threshold by crossing the street. I knew the team was nearby, and if Pre-Crisis was triggered, then I would make my way to them in a hasty manner. Fortunately, the men stayed on their side of the street. But, I noticed one of them was waving his arm to get my attention. I looked, and they both ran their extended thumbs across their necks, the international sign for "we want to cut your head off."

Threat confirmed! Pre-Crisis Mode activated. Decision made. I went right into Crisis Mode (act out decisions already made in Pre-Crisis). I acted upon the decision to find my team and make them aware of the problem.

I ducked into a shop where I had noticed one of my students pretending to be shopping. Seeing him was a huge relief. I discreetly informed him of the threats. He radioed the rest of the team, and we exited the shop together. The young men were not in sight, and we made our way back to the vehicles and then to the classroom. This reaction may seem extreme, but I can assure you, the environment was hostile. You never know how many threats there really are or if an ambush is already in place.

— — —

As this example demonstrates, a multilevel personal crisis management system can increase awareness, confirm threats, and prevent victimization, compromise and even death. The transfers from mode to mode (Alert, Pre-Crisis, and Crisis) depend heavily on two identified stages of the OODA loop, *observation* and *decision*. Both are instrumental in guiding the most effective action against a variety of threats.

In the following chapter, I will explore how your powers of observation and decision-making can be used to augment Situational Awareness and the Modes of Awareness cycle.

*"Don't tell me how educated you are,
tell me how much you traveled."* —Mohammed

Chapter 1 Review
Practice Assignment – Modes of Awareness Cycle

In this section, we've tackled the important concepts of Situational Awareness and the Modes of Awareness. Situational Awareness *is a conscious and constant focus on the environment* that seeks to detect, validate and confirm threats. Your ability to detect potential threats can result from natural instinct, but can also be developed as a skill. Situational Awareness is a habit of mind. Like any other, it takes time to develop and should be approached as a way of life.

As a way of practicing that skill, let's see how you would apply the Modes of Awareness and OODA concepts to the scenario below.

Practical Example

- Semi-permissive environment (area with limited government control)

- Visiting on assignment with a colleague who knows the local environment

In this scenario, you are traveling on assignment in Mexico. You've made arrangements with the local lead and feel comfortable with the information he has supplied. He picks you up at the Mexico City airport. Using Situational Awareness, you've done your homework and recognize that it will be important to be cautious because both American and Mexicans are vulnerable to crime and the risk of kidnapping in Mexico City.

During the ride from the airport, you discuss the overall security situation with your colleague, gaining additional information. Your associate drops you off at your hotel in a nice part of town. You are in **Alert Mode,** in the *observation* stage of the OODA loop process, scanning the environment for potential threats. You are orienting yourself to the environment both on the ride and as you survey your hotel room. You make a note of the individuals in the hotel, the check-in and checkout procedures, the fire emergency process and any potential threats.

After a successful meeting, you return to your hotel. In the lobby, a uniformed man approaches you. He stops you and indicates that he is with the local police force and needs to speak with you. You are still in Alert Mode and should be quickly analyzing this new information (*orient*).

Study Guide Questions

What should you do next? Are you still in Alert Mode? Why or why not?

Do you think this person is a threat? Why or why not? How would you determine this?

What do you think happens in this scenario?

Study Guide Answers

What should you do next? Are you still in Alert Mode? Why or why not?

Did you continue with your OODA loop process? The next step would be to make a *decision*—in the *Alert Mode* stage, you should be making key decisions, as there won't be much time for decision-making in the *Pre-Crisis* and *Crisis Modes*. You should also be setting the *invisible thresholds* that will determine a shift into Pre-Crisis mode. At this point, you are still in Alert Mode.

In this case, you might have done some homework before traveling and learned of recent incidents in which impersonators donned uniforms to perpetrate a crime. All that information is being pulled together in the *orient* step of the OODA loop. Given the environment, you decide that your invisible threshold will be breached if the individual tries to forcibly take you somewhere. Your instincts are telling you that something just doesn't seem right.

You are also making decisions at this point about what you will do if this person *does* try to take you somewhere. You are getting ready to *act*, to shift to Pre-Crisis, if the invisible threshold is crossed.

Do you think this person is a threat? Why or why not? How would you determine this?

Good research can help give you a head start about potential threats like this one. Instinct also comes into play. In this case, the uniformed individual grabs your arm and tries to move you toward the door of the hotel. He is saying something unintelligible about going to the police station. Yep, a *confirmed* threat. Your invisible threshold has been breached, and you shift into *Pre-Crisis Mode.*

What do you think happened in this scenario?

The uniformed individual begins to make a scene. Americans hate scenes, and most will comply with orders in order to put a halt to a heated interaction. But if you have quickly run through the Observe, Orient, Decide and Act process and determined the individual's behavior to be a trap, you will shift from *Pre-Crisis* to *Crisis Mode.* You will do the unexpected and *act* based on the decisions you made in Pre-Alert Mode.

You pull your arm away and walk quickly toward the hotel front desk. You pull out your cell phone and call your colleague. The uniformed individual comes after you. You remain calm but keep walking to stay ahead of him. You explain the situation to your colleague to make sure someone else knows what is happening.

You reach the hotel front desk, making sure a number of people are around as witnesses. You request assistance and explain you do not think this person is really a police officer. Suddenly, the uniformed individual disappears. The threat is over—for now. Your homework and your ability to analyze and respond quickly to a potential threat has served you well. What was it all about? Most likely, it was a potential kidnapping scheme. Thanks to thorough preparation, and the ability to process information quickly using the Modes of Awareness cycle and the OODA loop, you were able to elude this threat. Congratulations!

Lessons Learned:

- Research threats before traveling. Learn as much about the environment you are going into as possible.

- Use Situational Awareness, the Modes of Awareness cycle and the OODA loop to give you the advantage over potential threats. With these proven approaches and processes, you won't be frozen in place by the unanticipated and unexpected. You'll always be thinking ahead and ready to act.

NOTES:

References Chapter 1

Agan, R.D. (1987). Intuitive knowing as a dimension of nursing. Advances in Nursing Science, 10 (1), 63-70.

Atherton, J. (1999). Reflective Practice. Http://website.ntl.com.

Brockmann, E. N. & Anthony, W.P. (1998), The influence of tacit knowledge and collective mind on strategic planning. Journal of Managerial Issues, 10(2), 204-222.

Cannon-Bowers, J.A., Salas, E., & Pruitt, J.S. (1996). Establishing the boundaries of a paradigm for design-making research. (decision-making in complex environments) Human Factors, 38. 193-203.

Cohen, M.S. (1993). The naturalistic basis of decision biases. In G. A. Klein & J. Orsanu & R. Calderwood & C. Zsambok (eds). Decision-making in action: Models and methods. (pp. 50-99). Norwood, NJ: Ablex.

deBecker, G. (1997). The gift of fear. New York: Dell Publishing.

Grossman, D. & Christensen, L., "Of Sheep, Wolves, and Sheepdogs," Arkansas Lawman, June, 2005

Klein, G.A., Calderwood, R., & MacGregro, D. (1989). Critical decision method of eliciting knowledge. IEEE transactions on systems, man and cybernetics, 19, 462-472.

Morris, L.E. (1990). Strategies and tactics to access.

Polanyi, M. (1958). Personal knowledge. Chicago: The University of Chicago Press.

Randel, J.M., Pugh, L.H. & Reed, S.K. (1996). Differences in expert and novice situation awareness in naturalistic decision-making. International Journal of Human Computer Studies, 45, 579-597.

Schon, D.A. (1983). The reflective practitioner: How professionals think in action: Basic Books – Harper Collins.

Smithson, M. (1989). Ignorance and uncertainty: Emerging paradigms. New York: Springer Verlag.

Sternberg, R.J. & Horvath, J.A. (1999). Tactic knowledge in professional practice. Mahwah, NJ: Lawrence Erlbaum Associates, Inc. Publishers.

Surveillance Countermeasures, ACM 4 Security Services, Paladin Press, Boulder Colorado. 1994.

Chapter 2

Observation and Naturalistic Decision-Making

"A traveler without observation is a bird without wings."
—Moslih Eddin Saadi

This chapter examines how two important concepts can enhance your Situational Awareness and help you decide when to transition from one Mode of Awareness to another. The first is the power of observation. The second is a type of decision-making called Naturalistic Decision-Making (NDM).

The Power of Observation

Observation steers the Modes of Awareness cycle.

A skill that makes you a safer, more secure traveler, it helps you assess the environment, identify potential risks or threats, and find ways to avoid those threats, or plan avenues of escape. By focusing your mind on a particular element in your environment, whether it's a fact, event or person, observation allows you to recognize and retain that fact and recall it in the future. Highly dependent on the body's senses (sight, hearing, and to a lesser degree, smell), observation plays a critical role in a crisis.

Effective observation requires a conscious effort on your part. It consists of a keen ability to retain images of specific individuals, objects and occurrences. It's the perception of shapes, size and features. Colors, shades and lighting. Speed, time and distance. It consists of three processes: *attention, perception*, and *retention*.

Attention is most critical during the alert or pre-crisis mode. Without attention, perception and retention are impossible. Usually, your attention is limited to items and events with a direct bearing on your activity. If you are driving down the road, your attention is mostly focused on what's in front of you. Your involuntary attention may be captured by something out-of-the ordinary. For example, when you're walking through a crowd, a person with a limp may draw your attention. Very large or small people, bright colors, and sharp or loud sounds have the same effect. The Modes of Awareness cycle and the OODA loop will help broaden the range of your attention. This greater span of attention is important in building your Situational Awareness so you can identify potential threats.

Perception is heavily influenced by your experience, background and education. People tend to perceive and remember only the familiar or what interests them. Here again, your ability to expand observation beyond ingrained habits requires a conscious effort. Your mind will tend to filter out items subconsciously when you don't have a frame of reference to help retain them for subsequent retrieval. To improve your powers of observation, you'll want to be aware of these tendencies.

Retention must be practiced. People have a tendency to remember what they want and forget everything else. We need to train our brains, just like our bodies, to be adept at particular skills.

A couple of techniques can enhance your ability to retain details.

You can build skills using the mind-image association techniques that are practiced in Dale Carnegie seminars, along with other memory aids. These techniques stack strong imagery and mental associations with repetition, as follows:

- Create a strong mental *visual picture or association* with the item. It helps if the mental association is something that resonates with you, even if it's nonsensical to someone else. For example, if the person you want to remember looks like your 12th grade English teacher, then make that association. You'll remember that she had blonde hair and was slim, just like Mrs. Dye. It also helps to create an exaggerated caricature of the object and add an emotional connection by involving your five senses in the mental picture.

- To improve your recall, practice *serial association*:

  - Create a vivid mental picture for a list of items, say 15 or so, which you will have to recall in order. Exaggerate each item in terms of color and motion.

  - For example, take articles of clothing. Start with a tie, and have the tie be a vivid red color, which is choking someone, causing them to turn red in the face. Next up is a pair of green high heels, which you associate with a day-glo green color. The heels are slipping up and down, causing blisters on the person's feet. The third item might be a hat. Think of a French beret with a striking black-and-white hound's-tooth pattern, which is moving all around so that it causes you to feel dizzy.

- If you use this type of vivid imagery, associated with all five of your senses, it will be much easier to recall a long list of items, or the faces or names of individuals.

- *Repeat* the mental picture over and over, or say someone's name over and over.

Keep In Mind (KIM) drills are great for increasing observation and retention performance. This training drill is used in sniper-related military training and requires a partner to set up several different objects, in a particular order, spread out within a designated environment. You then have a limited amount of time to observe and retain the details of the pre-staged environment. Once the time is up, you must write down everything observed and sketch exactly where each item was located. Doing this regularly increases your ability to observe and retain small details.

As mentioned previously, you need to pay attention to perceive and retain information. Remember, too, that perception can play games with you. Most people use Hollywood and the media as their frame of reference for what a threat looks like. This type of reference limits you.

Often, real threats are unassuming and invisible in the environment. Don't filter out the real threats because of false stereotypes. Be as concerned about the baby-faced teenager who is hanging out (and probably eyeing your purse or wallet) as you are the hulking "foreigner."

Areas of Observation

Let's take a closer look at observation by breaking down all the identifiable information for a specific threat. Say the threat is surveillance, which is increasingly a real issue for business travelers. A businessperson may be watched by those who interested in proprietary company information or an unsavory character plotting a kidnapping for ransom. It happens more than you might think.

With surveillance detection, the primary objective is to identify or confirm that you are under surveillance. An example taken from my personal experience with surveillance detection helps to illustrate just how complicated that can be.

I was in a third-world country validating that a team was still conducting active surveillance of a particular country's embassy. Basically, locals were hired to "hang out" in the embassy vicinity and report any unusual behavior. Validating the team proved difficult because each member looked exactly the same. They were all clean-shaven Africans with well-groomed hair who wore slacks and collared shirts, drove taxis and mingled among other people with similar features and clothing. I couldn't stare at them as a crowd, or I would have been identified as a possible threat and reported. That would have been bad.

So, I had to find specific characteristics to identify each individual person. One guy wore the same shirt almost every day. Another always squatted in the same spot. Others I had to associate with the taxi they drove. This took weeks and was very difficult, which is a lot like trying to determine if you're being followed.

Identifying a multi-member surveillance team takes a considerable amount of observation, and involves the ability to retain the characteristics of these members even as they travel in a sea of other people. We will discuss this in more detail in future chapters, but for now, let's concentrate on what characteristics to retain.

If you're being followed, or suspect you're being followed, you will want to try to remember key characteristics about that person. This will help you confirm if you are encountering that same individual again and again, or if it's just people with similar characteristics. It's not feasible to remember everyone around you. You have to focus in on an individual's dominant characteristics, the ones that are difficult to alter. Don't waste time memorizing useless information. Develop an overall mental image of the individual, and key in on the retainable features. Once you start learning to categorize these features during observation, they become easier to retain and identify in the future.

The dominant **characteristics** to retain are *feature* and *form*. Body features consist primarily of face, head and hair. Three things that directly impact these are gender, race and age, although these are not considered features in and of themselves because none of them can stand alone as an identifiable characteristic for surveillance detection. Body features are the most accurate characteristics to help you to identify individuals. With exception of hair color, these are generally the most difficult and time consuming to alter. Body features, however, are the most difficult to observe because they require you to be close enough to scrutinize the individual. Take note of the following:

Dominant Identifying Characteristics			
Body Features			
Face	Head	Hair	Body Type/Build/Demeanor
Overall shape	Overall shape	Note: color can easily be changed	Heavy, stocky, medium or lean
Round, thin, square, broad, fat, thin or long	Round or Egg-shaped	Observe body hair, which is less easily changed	Tall, medium or short in height (or estimate in feet/inches)
(retainable for short duration) Wrinkles, scars, dimples, moles, overall complexion	High in crown	Especially focus on chest, arm and leg hair	Trunk features, arms, legs
Body fat or lack can impact face shape	Bulging in back or flat at back		Demeanor, especially mannerisms Posture, stride, pace of motion, voice quality Personality – introvert or extrovert
Physical (Longevity) Items			
Backpacks, purses, bags	Shoes	Watches	Belts

Observation of form includes the shape, build, and size of an individual. Any prominent physical aspect can be isolated for retention purposes. The overall body shape is made up of the trunk, arms, and legs. Keep in mind that how clothing fits can distort your perception of body shape. Size is relative to overall body shape but can be distorted by distance. Doors and doorways make great reference points when determining approximate height. Once again, distance can distort perception of height. Finally, posture can have a significant effect on overall form. This is a mannerism or demeanor trait.

A-H Guide to Make Identifying Human Threats Easier

A   **Age:** Young, Middle or Older

B   **Build:** Slender, Medium or Large

C   **Clothing:** Head to toe, hat, shirt, pants, shoes

D   **Distinguishing Marks:** tattoos, scars, moles, birthmarks

E   **Elevation or Height:** short, average, tall

F   **Face:** head shape, hair line, eyes, nose

G   **Gait:** posture, walk, stride, limps

H   **Hair:** color, length, thickness, lack of

Demeanor, particularly mannerisms, are characteristics or idiosyncrasies unique to an individual and easily retained. Peculiarities in action or bearing, mannerisms could be in posture, stride, pace of motion, or voice quality. Individual demeanor is established through myriad of mannerisms. These actions are either programmed over a lifetime or result from physical characteristics. Those developed over a lifetime become subconscious actions and therefore can only be controlled by conscious effort.

Mannerisms that result from physical characteristics are much more difficult to alter because the mind cannot control or conceal what the body is unable to. For this reason, mannerisms are one of the most important key traits to observe during surveillance. Most other traits can be concealed or disguised, but mannerisms take serious, conscience effort. Stride and posture are the easiest to observe and recognize again at a later location. Another is someone's personality trait. For example, extroverts display a more outgoing, positive or aggressive demeanor. These characteristics are difficult to disguise or conceal in the heat of surveillance.

Items people use and keep for a longer period of time, or **longevity items**, can also be observable points. These include things like backpacks, bags, shoes, purses, belts or other props a surveillance operator would wear or carry. Surveillance personnel may change clothes, disguises or wigs, but they very rarely will take time to change shoes, belts, purses or bags. Typically, surveillance personnel carry cameras and other technical devices. Switching gear from one bag to another is time consuming. Watches are also items to observe. Most surveillance operators wear watches and typically don't think to switch those out.

Aids to Help Identify Surveillance Vehicles

> **License Plate/Last 4:** color, country, numbers

> **Driver/Passengers:** description, gender, color

> **Dents/Damage:** size, location

> **Symbols/Stickers:** make, model, logo

Surveillance is only one threat of many where observation is key. If you thoroughly identify traits unique to a potential threat and retain the images for later use, you can piece together much of the overall threat picture.

Observation is a grossly overlooked, yet vital, element to survival. Observation steers transitions between Alert, Pre-Crisis, and Crisis modes, assesses the environment, identifies threats, and finds avenues of escape at which point a decision must be made.

Decision-Making

Let's now turn to the next element that drives the transition from one mode of awareness to another: **decisions.** I am not talking about ordinary, run-of-the-mill decisions, which are usually made with the luxury of time for clearly defined problems and in a relaxed environment. Rather, this is a specific subset of tactical decision-making, which is called **Naturalistic Decision-Making (NDM).**

By definition, Naturalistic Decision-Making is used when: stakes are high, time is crunched, and stress is abundant. Decisions drive actions, and those actions determine your ability to be a safe and secure world traveler.

Dr. Michael Uttaro, retired FBI agent and chief executive officer of Tactical Operations Support Services, is a subject matter expert on this type of decision-making. His research lays out the scientific aspects of Naturalistic Decision-Making. You will note how NDM supports Situational Awareness as defined under the Total Awareness system.

Naturalistic Decision-Making

Uttaro states that every day, we "make a number of decisions which, when placed on a continuum, range from very easy to extremely difficult. Many of these decisions can be considered routine and are made in a manner that does not require a considerable amount of thought or effort. Other decisions, however, require intensive deliberation; their consequences have a profound influence over many lives. Take, for example, the decision-making associated with the aftermath of September 11th, and the lives affected by the decisions that readied this nation for war. It is these types of judgments and decisions that most interest researchers.

"This new paradigm, labeled 'naturalistic decision-making,' provides a description of decision-making as it unfolds in a field setting and 'rejects a purely formal approach, whether for describing or for evaluating decisions.'"

Uttaro and others are seeking to understand how complex decisions are best made in demanding situations. The field of naturalistic decision-making focuses on situational awareness, planning and other cognitive functions that emerge in natural settings instead of in a controlled laboratory setting. This type of decision-making is critical in occupations such as air traffic control, the military, fire fighting, surgery and others where high-risk decisions need to be made quickly. I've bolded some of the text in the quotes below to highlight some of the key points about NDM:

As Uttaro goes on to say, "Under true conditions, you often avoid situations that are ambiguous and in a state of chaos and disorder. **To better make a decision, the recognition of detail is accomplished mainly by observation**, which gets contextual meaning through the analytical and intuitive processes.

"Another decision making tool, 'intuitive messenger,' is the ubiquitous hunches or "gut feelings" that are so often associated with effective policing. **Research has shown that intuition, as a whole, strongly influences one's decision-making/judgment competency and proficiency.** [. . .] One problem lies in our inability to properly listen to these omnipresent intuitive signals when rendering decisions. The consequence of ignoring the 'intuitive messengers' during criminal encounters could prove costly for victims and officers because **calm, thoughtful, and rational decision-making can hardly function under situations of violence and uncertainty.**

"With intuition representing one side of the decision-making (judgment) continuum, a more systematic and analytical approach for coping with uncertainty represents the other...

"Although this approach or strategy would be difficult to implement during acts of violence, it does offer the more 'classical,' rational process for dealing with uncertainty in the decision-making process, and emphasizes the need to gain full information of the situation. Additionally, **decision-makers under real world conditions realize that there is an appropriate proportion between the time needed to reflect on a condition and the action required to resolve that condition.** The appropriate proportion for each, reflection and action, will vary from situation to situation...

"Decision-making research has undergone a shift from the 'classical' to 'naturalistic' perspective, given the importance of decision-making to real-world problems and the impact it has on how the field might advance.

"The dynamics that influence decision-making under true operational conditions become stressed because the context of the moment is constantly undergoing change.

"In naturalistic settings with time constraints, changing conditions, and stress related influences; recognition-primed decisions (RPD) are hypothesized to take the place that involve an assessment of the situation, recognition of the events as typical, and a resultant course of action based on previous experience. An RPD is **distinguished from classical decision models by focusing on the assessment of the situation, rather than assessing different**

courses of action and judging one option superior to others.
The RPD model emphasizes the recognition of situational dynamics and relies on the experience of the decision-maker to determine what course of action is appropriate."

Decision-Making Preparation

One factor that contributes greatly towards the effectiveness of the decision-making process is extensive preparation. The Total Awareness system is all about being prepared.

As Uttaro goes on to say, "**Preparation is considered a fundamental task, essential in producing positive results, but is often overlooked or at least neglected.** Preparation is the filling in of the details, the development of possible routes, the recognition of potential barriers, and the construction of options."

Without preparation, you are left to draw only on *experience*, and you react in an information vacuum. This limits your options to those that are immediately at hand. Experience, or more appropriately, a lack of experience, limits the skill set needed to anticipate and react to a "surprise."

Though in the heat of the moment, it can never adequately substitute for the preparation of a range of potential responses, experience can greatly assist in the development of 'what if's' and in the construction of worst-case scenarios. These worst-case scenarios are the trigger points, or barriers, that cause you to change course or shift modes during a dynamic event.

Preparation involves several stages, including activities undertaken prior to your trip and activities that can be done while traveling. Before traveling, you need to gather as much knowledge and awareness about the location or impending situation as possible. This is critical because the smallest detail could prove very beneficial when barriers are encountered and alternatives need to be explored. Before making decisions, you will want to note everything you can about the surroundings. This allows you to understand all the potential options should you need to take advantage of them. One way you can accomplish this is to create as many worst-case scenarios as possible and think though the consequences associated with each scenario. This also serves as a preventive mechanism to avoid potentially bad decisions when action is eventually required.

This level of detail provides the input that you will need to construct an internal cognitive map. Unanticipated or unpredicted scenarios do occur in real life. How ready will you be to respond to these events? That will depend on how thoroughly you have prepared, how often you have reviewed and evaluated the ongoing and unfolding "situation."

By providing this incessant inspection and assembling suitable details of the scanned and stored data, barriers will be quickly observed and corresponding routes will soon emerge. By increasing your awareness, you will be better equipped to perform the constant scanning that is needed to update your knowledge as the scenario unfolds. These scans provide the information you need to help determine your available options. Then, you can then use threat mitigation alternatives by examining the possible benefits of a change in tactics. At the same time, you will also be seeking ways to reduce the threat.

Decision-making is about more than what shoes are to be worn for the day, especially when the wolf comes prowling.

> "I come in here and the first thing I'm doing is catching the sidelines and looking for an exit...I can tell you the license plate on all six cars outside; our waitress is left-handed and the guy sitting up at the counter is 215 pounds and knows how to handle himself. I know the best place to look for a gun is in the cab of the gray truck outside. And at this altitude I can run flat-out for a half mile before my hands start to shake. Why would I know that?" —Jason Bourne, *Bourne Identity 2002.*

If only it were that simple!

> *"The first condition of understanding a foreign country is to smell it."* —Rudyard Kipling

Chapter 2 Review
Practice Assignment – Observation and Naturalistic Decision-Making

How Powers of Observation Can Save Your Wallet and a Lot More

In this chapter, we've explored how observation and Naturalistic Decision-Making can help enhance your awareness of the environment around you. Now, let's apply those skills to a hypothetical situation.

Practical Example

- Semi-permissive environment (area with some government control)

- Family vacation

When I was a kid, my dad worked in Saudi Arabia for ARAMCO, one of the most powerful oil companies in the world. Every year the company provided employees with $5,000 dollars per family member to go on vacation for 30 days, which was not a bad deal. The real reason for the stipend was to give us a chance to renew our visas. (The Saudis would only allow foreigners 11-month visas. Don't ask me why—no clue.)

One summer, we ended up in Rome. It was incredibly hot. My dad enjoyed walking everywhere, although the rest of the family (me, my mom and little brother) would have preferred a taxi. This particular day, we were walking toward St. Peter's Basilica to see the Pope perform his daily ritual of water sprinkling, hand waving and baby kissing.

We trudged on in the scorching heat. Drops of sweat rolled off our skin. As we crossed a bridge, our little family passed a group of about ten Gypsy children, ranging in age from about six to ten years. They were playing sidewalk games. As we approached, the children started crying and begging for money, food and water. They began to tug on me, my mom, the stroller (with my brother in it) and my dad, all the while, making signs for food, water and money. The minute we passed through their gauntlet, the crowd went quiet.

Suddenly my dad started to yell, "They took my wallet!"

He forced them to the wall of the bridge and continued to shout, "Wallet, wallet, give me my wallet!"

My mom then started to scream, "Polieeze, polieeze!"

My dad turned to me and bellowed, "Clint, start kicking their butts!"

I was nine. I just maintained the stroller with my brother inside and watched my parents freak out. Entertaining to say the least.

Eventually, the wallet came flying from the center of the crowd of kids and landed on the sidewalk. The cop on the corner just watched. The world loves Americans!

Study Guide Questions

How did my dad know his wallet had been taken? After all, the begging and tugging were great distractions.

Let's do a little quiz to see how well you recall some of the details of the scene I just described. How many Gypsy children were there? What was their approximate age range? What time of year was it? How many people were in my family? Who were they? How old was I? What did the policeman do?

Study Guide Answers

How did my dad know his wallet had been taken?

How did my dad know that his wallet had been taken? It was because he was literally sweating his butt off. The cool breeze that suddenly visited his back pocket cued him immediately. He was using one of his five senses, his sense of feel. This power of observation helped our family out and saved his wallet—and its contents.

After that, my dad came up with a great anti-pickpocket trick. Dad always carried a pocket comb to tidy up his little remaining hair. He inserted the plastic comb length wise in the fold of his bi-fold wallet with the teeth up. That simple move made it impossible for the wallet to come out of his pocket without the comb teeth getting hung up on the pocket interior. It was great fun watching him pay for stuff. Every time he had to extract his wallet from his back pocket, he would tug away and curse the whole time, but his wallet was always there.

Recall quiz: How many Gypsy children were there? What was their approximate age range? What time of year was it? How many people were in my family? Who were they? How old was I? What did the policeman do?

Now about that quiz to build your powers of recall. There were ten kids from about six to ten years in age. It was summer—did the details about the sweat help you remember that part? There were four people in my family: my dad, mom, my little brother and me. I was nine. And the policeman, he just watched the show.

With practice, you'll be able to enhance powers of observation and decision-making. Those skills can come in very handy in helping you detect potential threats while you are traveling—but they can be just as important when you are in your hometown or negotiating at a business meeting.

NOTES:

References Chapter 2

Agan, R.D. (1987). Intuitive knowing as a dimension of nursing. Advances in Nursing Science, 10 (1), 63-70.

Atherton, J. (1999). Reflective Practice. Http://website.ntl.com.

Brockmann, E. N. & Anthony, W.P. (1998), The influence of tacit knowledge and collective mind on strategic planning. Journal of Managerial Issues, 10(2), 204-222.

Cannon-Bowers, J.A., Salas, E., & Pruitt, J.S. (1996). Establishing the boundaries of a paradigm for design-making research. (decision-making in complex environments) Human Factors, 38. 193-203.

Cohen, M.S. (1993). The naturalistic basis of decision biases. In G. A. Klein & J. Orsanu & R. Calderwood & C. Zsambok (eds). Decision-making in action: Models and methods. (pp. 50-99). Norwood, NJ: Ablex.

deBecker, G. (1997). The gift of fear. New York: Dell Publishing.

Grossman, D. & Christensen, L., "Of Sheep, Wolves, and Sheepdogs," Arkansas Lawman, June, 2005

Klein, G.A. (1997). The recognition-primed decision (RPD) model: Looking back, looking forward. In C. Zsambok & G.A. Klein (eds.), Naturalistic decision-making. Mahwah, NJ: Lawrence Erlbaum Associates, Inc.

Klein, G.A., Calderwood, R., & MacGregro, D. (1989). Critical decision method of eliciting knowledge. IEEE transactions on systems, man and cybernetics, 19, 462-472.

Morris, L.E. (1990). Strategies and tactics to access.

Polanyi, M. (1958). Personal knowledge. Chicago: The University of Chicago Press.

Randel, J.M., Pugh, L.H. & Reed, S.K. (1996). Differences in expert and novice situation awareness in naturalistic decision-making. International Journal of Human Computer Studies, 45, 579-597.

Schon, D.A. (1983). The reflective practitioner: How professionals think in action: Basic Books – Harper Collins.

Smithson, M. (1989). Ignorance and uncertainty: Emerging paradigms. New York: Springer Verlag.

Sternberg, R.J. & Horvath, J.A. (1999). Tactic knowledge in professional practice. Mahwah, NJ: Lawrence Erlbaum Associates, Inc. Publishers.

Surveillance Countermeasures, ACM 4 Security Services, Paladin Press, Boulder Colorado. 1994.

Uttaro, Michael. "NATURALISTIC decision-making in law enforcement practice – EXPLORING THE PROCESS, Dissertation. 2002 Falls Church, VA.

Chapter 3

Personal Awareness

"Travel can be one of the most rewarding forms of introspection."
—Lawrence Durrell

Personal Awareness (PA) is the image and demeanor you project to the public.

You have the ability to increase your own self-awareness, and as a result, manage how you are perceived. This power allows you to blend in within a specific culture, reducing threat vulnerabilities and keeping you off the radar of criminals, other bad guys and the general public (Third Party Awareness). Personal Awareness is the most important aspect of the Total Awareness system. It should always be guided by the culture of your destination.

Using Personal Awareness, you will assess and manage specific character traits that might separate you from the culture you will be visiting. You will need to identify your personal vulnerabilities and exposures based on the host country environment. What do I mean by personal vulnerabilities and exposures? The following example provides a good illustration.

When Sheepdogs Must Dress Like Sheep

During World War II, a joint operation was launched in Nazi-occupied territories. British Special Operations Executive, the U.S. Office of Strategic

Services, and the French Bureau Central de Renseignements et d'Action together conducted sabotage and guerrilla warfare, and led the French Foreign Resistance. These operations were directed by three-man teams, usually composed of an American, French and British operative. The three-man multinational unit would parachute into enemy territory to train, equip, organize and lead pockets of civilians on raids against Nazi targets. These operations were code-named "Jedburgh."

Such missions required a very deliberate and thorough training pipeline. Most volunteers were seasoned World War II soldiers with combat experience, language skills, radio operator experience and leadership skills. The training consisted of parachuting, land navigation, clandestine radio operations, weapons, explosives, tactics, and basic tradecraft (also known as spycraft). Although the training was exceptional for its time, it lacked a few valuable life-saving skills that would have helped these operatives blend into the local environments.

In some areas of operation, Jedburgh team members had to pose as French citizens, living, working and eating together with Nazis. The Jedburgh members had to dress, walk, smell, and eat like Frenchmen—which was completely foreign to the American and British operatives. Because of this deficiency, several Jedburgh team members were identified as "different," questioned, taken prisoner, or executed on the spot.

One interview revealed that the Americans were unfamiliar with European dining customs. Americans hold their fork with their right hand and usually leave the knife on the table until it is required. When cutting, Americans switch the fork from their right to their left hand, pick up the knife with the right, and cut their food. When not cutting, the knife is put down, and the fork is used to carry the food to the mouth. Europeans use both the knife and fork the entire meal and never switch positions. Simple, little mistakes like this cost lives.

Similarly, the British operatives couldn't break the habit of pouring milk in their cup before adding hot tea. Other Europeans pour the hot tea into a cup first and then add milk. Knowing and using these local customs would have saved lives.

The Jedburghs were victims of personal habit and cultural difference. The saying, "It's the little things," truly applies to this example. To break lifelong habits is difficult. Instead of trying to quit, it is sometimes easier to just replace your distinctively different habit with another that fits into the local culture. Creating a new habit takes some effort. It takes eight days of constant reminders for 90 percent retention, 21 days to start a pattern, and 100 days for a new action to become automatic. So don't think that those two days of practice prior to departure are going to set you up for success.

Why Disguise is Important

You may not be a clandestine operative, but you *will* be scrutinized and judged everywhere you travel. You may think, "Why bother? I am the opposite color of the people at my destination. I am going to stand out anyway."

That may be an accurate statement. The observing party, however, doesn't necessarily know that you are American. You could appear, based on appearance and actions, European, Canadian, Australian or South African. Bottom line, Americans are unfortunately more frequently targeted than some other nationalities. Toning down your American signatures will help reduce your vulnerabilities.

You have to live and breathe awareness through daily action, whether you are in the comfort of your own home or traveling abroad. Proper planning, research and the constant injection of awareness into your daily life are a must. If an action is part of your lifestyle, it will appear natural to third parties when you are traveling in different environments.

Remember John Boyd, who developed the OODA loop, from Chapter 1? I want to highlight some of Boyd's thoughts on warfare. He divided warfare into three distinct elements: *moral warfare, mental warfare* and *physical warfare. Moral warfare* destroys the enemy's will to win and breaks down fibers of trust within a unit. *Mental warfare* distorts the enemy's perception of reality through disinformation, posturing and projection. Finally, *physical warfare* is the destruction of the enemy, enemy resources and other assets.

Your projection and demeanor, a crucial part of Personal Awareness, is a form of mental warfare. Now, you may be a peace-loving person. You are probably thinking, "I don't want to wage war on anyone, and I certainly don't want to pick a fight when I am traveling abroad." Those things may be true, but that's not the point. We are talking about using deception to distort the perception of potential predator—this is a form of preventive mental warfare.

In any case, this form of warfare sometimes involves acting meeker than you really are. Sometimes it pays for a sheepdog to pose as a sheep. Are there instances where this could give you the advantage? You better believe it. Presenting yourself as a tough guy might ward off wolves in Los Angeles, but my guess is that it wouldn't work in northern Pakistan. This is where I would employ the sheep, sheepdog and wolf differently than Grossman. There are times when you must look like a sheepdog to ward off wolves. But when traveling with an array of sheep, or possibly having wolves around you, it might be more beneficial to look like a sheep.

I am not implying that your mindset should change to that of a sheep, but that you may want to consider projecting or presenting yourself as a sheep to reduce your threat vulnerabilities. In times of extreme crisis, however, you must become the wolf.

Though downgrading aggression may sound easier than ramping it up, I must identify the single most important issue sheepdogs or alpha types will face. EGO! Americans, as a whole, are very egotistical. Collapsing the ego and pretending to become a sheep is the most difficult task at hand for many of us. Vanity must be set aside. We all want to look pretty, or cool or tough, but these presentations will make us targets. Unless of course, you like that kind of attention. Then, by all means, start your day in an orange jumpsuit!

Remember, this book is dedicated to reducing your vulnerabilities and increasing your awareness across the board. Whether you are a diplomat, government operative or business traveler, blending in is better than standing out.

I tell students, all alpha males and gods in their own worlds, to put on penny loafers and a calculator watch, stop using hair products, and start wearing clothes from Goodwill. The looks I get are always the same—"no f*%#ing way" written all over their faces. But by the end of the course, they're usually ready to listen to me.

Beyond clothing, ego also drives physical posture, the way you walk, and your general aura. Some walk very confidently. Others walk like they're on a mission. Some walk as if they are superior. All of these traits are driven by ego. They are hard habits to break, but they can be broken through self-discipline. Change your habits. Your ego will follow.

So, here it is in a nutshell. You can reduce your threat vulnerabilities through sustained awareness, projection and demeanor management. That's it.

The Jedburgh teams of yesterday and the clandestine operatives of today understand the importance of cultural immersion. If you can't do an immersion trip, then research is the next best option. Country studies—researching pertinent country-specific issues, history, politics, culture, threats and so on—should be undertaken prior to departure. That's what separates the Total Awareness system from the rest—the commitment to studying the environment, its culture, its threats, and consolidating it all into your awareness profile. In Chapter 4 and the Appendices, you'll find a series of country guides, broken down by projection and demeanor, to help you blend in more effectively.

The Components of Personal Awareness

First, we are going to more fully explore how Personal Awareness—and its specific components, such as physical appearance and actions—can dramatically reduce your visibility.

The category of **physical appearance/projection** consists of, but is not limited to: clothing, jewelry, technology, grooming standards, gender, race and accessories, that the general public can observe and judge.

I have broken *projection* into *first-, second-* and *third-line gear*, which are terms that I've borrowed from the military. The terms refer to the layers of gear that a soldier wears into combat. The military would define first-line gear as items required to survive: the clothes you're wearing, a map, compass, first-aid kit, pistol and so on. Second-line gear would be your fighting gear, which includes your rifle, load bearing gear, bullets, communication equipment and night vision goggles. Third-line gear includes your backpack and its contents. Here is how I define these lines of gear in relation to the global traveler and Personal Awareness:

- *First-line gear* is difficult to change—it's your birthday suit. That's right, the bare-naked truth standing in the mirror looking back at you, waiting for constructive criticism. You want to identify any characteristics that are culturally offensive, would make you stand out in a crowd, or might make you a threat. Specific traits to pay attention to are gender, race, hair color, eye color, skin color, piercings, tattoos, circumcision and any gross abnormalities. Most of these traits cannot be changed, but all of them must be evaluated against the culture of the country you intend to visit. If caught by a wolf, you need to have a story explaining any irregularities that might be offensive or upsetting. For example, piercings such as trendy nose rings could make you more of a target than you know. Such a piercing on a man could offend a Hindi woman. Nose rings in India honor the marriage goddess, Parvathi.

- **Second-line gear** is easy to change—it's anything that touches your skin. Items like hats, sunglasses, shirts, pants, underwear, socks, gloves, necklaces, bracelets, watches and rings make up a large portion of the physical traits that define a person and may be used to distinguish you from others. Although this is the easiest line of gear to change, most will not. Americans want to look good, smell good and be noticed. But second-line gear is what provides identity and separates people from one another. Loud clothes with logos, brand names, and symbols give rifle sights a place to line up. Subdued second-line gear can make you look like a sheep and help you blend in with the flock.

- **Third-line gear** is anything that touches your clothes. This includes items like jackets, shoes, belts, man bags, purses, backpacks, wallets, passports, mobile phones and laptops. These are items that people use for long periods of time (longevity items) or have in limited quantities when traveling. They make tracking and surveillance easy. (As I mentioned and will continue to discuss, the wolf comes in many forms, and surveillance may be one of them.)

Demeanor is a category defined as physical actions, consisting of components like gestures, manners, language, your handshake, your walk and the way you talk. Chapter 4 is dedicated to country-specific appropriate actions and demeanor traits that you should use during travel to blend into specific cultures. For this discussion, I have broken demeanor or actions into three major categories: *body language, verbal language* and *protocol.*

- **Body Language** is defined as non-verbal physical movements and expressions that communicate intentional or non-intentional thoughts and emotions. A simple, yet powerful body language signal is a person crossing his or her arms. Other than signaling the person is physically cold, this gesture may typically indicate an unconscious barrier has been raised.

- **Verbal Language** is defined as verbal interaction where two or more parties exchange information. Verbal communication includes tone, word choice and language.

- **Protocol** is defined as international rules and social behavior, which includes body language and communication that are in accordance with a specific culture. Protocol includes greetings, manners and other actions that conform to a culture norm.

Now that you have the gist of Personal Awareness and the terms associated, you are ready to learn some specifics.

Don't Be the Ugly American

The term "ugly American" was most recently introduced to the world by our friends in Hollywood with the movie based on a novel co-written by William Lederer.

The Ugly American was about an ignorant, incompetent American traveling through a fictitious Asian country. In the novel, a Burmese journalist says, "For some reason, the [American] people I meet in my country are not the same as the ones I knew in the United States. A mysterious change seems to come over Americans when they go to a foreign land. They isolate themselves socially. They live pretentiously. They're loud and ostentatious."

Not too far from the truth. Americans need to learn to treat travel like they are going to a party at the boss's house. You should dress appropriately, eat differently, talk differently and be respectful to others at the party. Given the recent anti-American sentiment expressed in some countries and groups, you don't want to be the ugly American!

Some elements of projection and demeanor are entirely out of your control, but that means you should pay very close attention to what is within your sphere of influence. Skin color, eye color, and sex are not easily changed. Demeanor, or the way in which you act or carry yourself, however, is just as much a part of you as your race or sex. The small details—your clothing, accessories, and your actions—are completely controllable.

Jason Bourne knew this lesson all too well. The clandestine assassin, a fictional character in a series of Robert Ludlum novels, navigated his way through third-party surveillance and pursuit in foreign counties with snakelike ease. He moved through train stations, airports, streets and all of Europe by becoming a sheep. He dressed in muted colors, spoke the language, and became part of his environment. He was, simply, a chameleon.

Most of us aren't Jason Bournes. We're Clark W. Griswolds, the fictional character in the Vacation movie series. A proud American father, Clark pulled on his favorite "Wally World" sweatshirt, grabbed a Chicago Bears baseball cap, and took his family on vacation to Europe. You and Clark have the same thought in your head, "I'm a proud American, and I'm going to show it."

Although these two fictional characters represent extreme ends of the projection and demeanor trait spectrum, they provide important lessons. Be more like Jason, and less like Clark.

The accompanying chart provides a quick snapshot of innocent, yet important tip-offs that will draw unwanted attention to you in your world travels. You'll want to suppress these common American traits to blend in with the local culture and help ensure secure, safe travel:

Identifiers that Signal "The Ugly American"

Asking for Coke Expensive watches

Asking for ketchup	Wearing athletic shoes
Asking for ice	Wearing flip flops
Baseball caps	Wearing blue jeans
Sunglasses	Patriotic clothing
High-dollar tech devices	University, college, high-school clothing
Smokeless tobacco	Loud conversations
Chewing gum	

There are dozens of additional examples of how Americans inadvertently make themselves stand out and become easy targets. Like the Jedburghs and Griswolds, we all need to learn some new customs to blend in a bit better. It's smart, and it's also good manners.

Let's start with an etiquette lesson.

Etiquette Basics

Etiquette used to mean "keep off the grass." When Louis XIV's gardener at the French court of Versailles discovered that aristocrats were trampling through his gardens, he put signs up, or *etiquettes*, to warn them off. But the dukes and duchesses walked right past them anyway. Finally, the king himself had to decree that no one was to go beyond the bounds of the etiquettes. The term "etiquette" was expanded to mean a ticket to court functions that listed rules on where to stand and what to do. Like language, etiquette evolves, but in a sense, it still means "keep off the grass."

Teaching good manners was considered part of a child's upbringing until the 1960s—public and private schools actually used to include etiquette as part of a well-rounded curriculum. But the liberated '60s and '70s brought a decline in general manners in America. What does this have to do with escaping the wolf? Well, what Americans consider posh or fancy manners are the norm in most countries. We basically eat like slobs in comparison to European colonized populations.

In business and government arenas today, the term, "protocol," is often used instead of etiquette because it sounds more businesslike and official.

> "Eating is not an executive skill...but it is especially hard to imagine why anyone negotiating items of importance would consider it possible to skip mastering the very simple requirements...what else did they skip learning?" —Fortune 500 CEO

Noted. You can be the most articulate, well-dressed professional in the room, but if your manners are lacking, especially when dealing with ambassadors and the like, then your true professionalism will be questioned. Let's dig deeper into manners and etiquette to understand how you can use these to blend into the local culture.

Posture at the Table

Sit straight, but not stiff, against the back of the chair and rest both feet flat on the ground. Note: you are not straddling the chair, ready to leap out of it and fight someone.

Elbows should be kept close to your sides when eating. Move them forward and backward to convey the food to the mouth and to manipulate utensils. Note, your elbows are not bowed out with armpits exposed to the world.

Continental or European standards hold that both hands stay above the table at all times. It is considered rude to have one hand down on your lap and the other above. This custom is centuries-old, when a hand under the table was considered a threat, indicating that the diner was reaching for a weapon. This is hard for members of the military, who are used to eating fast in tight quarters where it is easier to put one arm under the table.

It should go without saying that in many cultures, nose blowing at the table is considered offensive. Any bodily functions should be taken care of away from the table.

The American Style of Eating

American-style eating is what mom and dad probably taught you, if they taught you at all. I will never forget eating for the first time with a very good friend of mine. He is highly educated, highly intelligent and culturally savvy. But he held his fork and knife with fists. He buried his face in his plate and went for it, maybe coming up for air a couple of times. At the end, the table was covered in crumbs, meat particles and spill marks. His mom and dad forgot that lesson, and he was born in the '60s. So if you were taught, it would have been something like this:

- The knife is only used for cutting

- The fork does most of the work and is held in the right hand like a pencil (tines, the points of the fork, are pointed up)

- When cutting, the knife is held with the right hand, and the fork is positioned in the left hand

- One piece cut at a time

- Once done cutting, the knife is put on the plate, the fork switched back to the right hand

- Food is conveyed to the mouth

That's pretty much what led to the murders of OSS operatives during World War II.

The Continental Style of Eating

In 1853, a French etiquette book confided that those that wish to eat fashionably should not change their fork from their right hand after they have cut their meat, but raise the meat to their mouth using their left hand. Before long, Europeans of all classes began eating in this way. Not to mention, it is more efficient to eat Continental style.

The Continental style of eating is becoming more and more popular in the United States. This is a "must" tactic when blending in overseas. Note the differences between Continental and American.

- The knife is held in the right hand for most of the meal and used to help the fork

- The fork is in the left hand with tines pointed down. The fork is essentially upside down for the entire meal

- The knife and fork are both held so that your index figures are pointing at the food

- When cutting, the fork and knife remain in original hands

- Food is conveyed to the mouth, tines down

Asian Style of Eating (Chopsticks)

Besides eating the entire meal with chopsticks, there are some interesting points to highlight:

- Never stand or stab your chopsticks into a bowl of rice

- Never point your chopsticks at someone

- Do remember to use the large ends of the chopsticks to serve yourself from a community platter

- Never eat directly from the platter, always place the food on your plate first

- Don't cross the chopsticks. When not in use, place the chopsticks side by side on the chopstick rest

General Overseas Dining Dos and Don'ts

- Do try everything served at least once

- Do avoid talking with your mouth full

- Do wait until you are done swallowing before taking a sip of water

- Do remember solids (food) are always on your left and fluids are on the right

- Do remember BMW—*bread, meal, water* in that order from left to right, so that you don't mistakenly use another person's glass or bread plate

- Do look into the drink not over it when drinking

- Don't overload your plate

- Don't overload your fork

- Don't mop your face with the napkin

- Don't throw your napkin on the dish when done

- Don't spread your elbows when cutting meat

- Don't saw the meat

- Don't chew with your mouth open

- Don't touch your face or head at the table

- Don't pick your teeth at the table

- Don't push your plate away when done

- Don't gesture with your utensils

- Don't eat your neighbor's bread (bread, milk, water, left to right)

Putting It All Together

The Total Awareness concept is more than just understanding your environment through your senses. A Total Awareness approach requires you to research and understand the location you are going to encounter. Ask yourself, am I going to a semi-permissive or non-permissive environment? What threats exist? What do I need to know before I go? We'll discuss those issues in the following chapters. For now, it's important that you understand that the environment drives the awareness layers.

"Travelers never think that they are the foreigners."
—Mason Cooley

Chapter 3 Review
Practice Assignment – Personal Awareness

When to NOT Be an Ugly American and When It Might Be Okay

In this chapter, we've explored how to blend in. It's the little things that often create cultural challenges when traveling abroad and betray your country of origin—choices in wardrobe, menu selections and habits that literally shout your national origin.

As discussed, you'll achieve your business objectives and attract less attention from unsavory characters by blending in and taking charge.

Practical Example

- Non-permissive environment (area with little/no government control)

- Shopping in a town

Good intentions don't always produce good results. Local resident Jamel thought he would ensure my safety by introducing me to curious locals as a Swedish veterinarian without informing me. Why Swedish, I asked him later. "Everyone loves Swedish people," he replied. I thought, no harm, no foul—until the next day, when I awoke to the sound of angry cries and the thump of rocks hitting my crude cinder block lodgings. What at first glance seemed to be only five to ten people were more than 100 when I was fully awake.

My local hosts were yelling, "Leave, leave! We go now, hurry, please!" Fortunately, I was already scheduled to depart that day. We escaped out the back of the compound in Land Cruisers and went at top speed the eight kilometers to the waiting aircraft on the dirt strip where the pilot of the Fokker 60 asked what I did to tick off half the population.

Study Guide Questions

Why do you think the local population was angry?

What could I have done earlier to change the outcome of this encounter?

Study Guide Answers

Why do you think the local population was angry?

I had no clue why the local community was up in arms—literally—until I found out the next day that a Swedish cartoonist named Lars Vilks had recently decided to sketch the Prophet Mohammed with the body of the dog, which was taken as a major insult by most of the Islamic world. Talk about bad timing.

What could I have done earlier to change the outcome of this encounter?

Lessons Learned:

- Control your guides or liaisons in country, and have a plan before you go out. In my case, Jamel was trying to be helpful, but no answer is sometimes the best answer.

- That would have been a good trip to be the "Ugly American" verses the "Handsome Swede."

- Don't think that speaking English identifies you as an American. Believe it or not, English truly is the international language. Americans, Australians and Brits can usually tell each other apart by accent, but the rest of the broken-English world often cannot tell where you are from.

If direct questions are asked, answer with a broad brush (macro to micro) and flip. Sample dialogue:

"Where are you from?"

"I am on holiday. Where are you from? How much for the hookah?"

Then, control the conversation from there.

Most people, regardless of culture, like to talk about themselves and their culture and provide helpful information. Oh, and of course, try and sell you inflatable Hello Kitty swimming pool rafts (weird, no water or swimming pools for hundreds of miles).

Last, but not least: If you're in a dangerous area, don't go walking around town.

NOTES:

References Chapter 3

Bosrock, Many Murray. Asian Business Customs & Manners, Meadow Brook Press, 5451 Smetana Drive, Minnetonka, Minnetonka, Minnesota. 2007.

Eyring, Pamela. The Protocol School of Washington Curriculum, Washington D.C., 2008.

Irwin, Will. The Jedburghs, the secret history of allied forces, France, 1944, Public Affairs/Perseus Book Group, New York, NY, 2005.

Chapter 4

Cultural Awareness

*"If you reject the food, ignore the customs,
fear the religion and avoid the people,
you might better stay at home."*
—James Michener

You are trying to blend in at micro levels in a foreign country. You may have the wrong skin tone, but at first glance, you don't necessarily have to be American. As discussed in the preceding chapter on Personal Awareness, you can minimize personal traits to call less attention to yourself so you don't stand out as an American. Conversely, you can take steps to blend into the local culture.

Cultural Awareness (CA) is the assessment and understanding of a specific geographic location's culture, including cultural-specific social protocol and etiquette but going all the way to mannerisms and gestures. As I will continue to stress, it's up to you to take ownership of any journey you embark on. Using the following list as an outline, take time to learn about the people and culture of your future destinations to increase awareness and make the most of your trip:

1. County, City

2. Basic History

3. Language

4. Initial Meeting Criteria

5. Dining Protocol

6. Projection

7. Demeanor

8. Business Meeting Criteria

9. Negotiation

10. Special Culture Specifics

Research aside, there are commonalities to practicing Cultural Awareness in any culture you visit:

- Conservative, muted business casual clothing is acceptable in most cultures.

- European table demeanor will work in almost any environment.

Although you should research more complete details on specific cultures, let's take a brief look at some subtle, and not so subtle, differences.

Handshaking Intelligence

- Australia – Firm grip with two strokes

- Belgium – Light pressure and quick stroke

- China – Light grip may include pumping, which shows pleasure in the greeting

- France – Light grip with a brisk stroke

- Germany – Firm grip and one stroke

- Japan – Light grip with three or four light strokes

- Korea – Medium firm handshake. To show respect when shaking hands, support your right forearm with your left hand

- Latin and South America – Light grip that lingers twice as long as the U.S. handshake

- Middle East – Limp and lingering grip with only a slight up and down movement, never stroke

- Sweden – Firm grip with one brisk stroke

- U.S. – Firm, solid grip with two or three stokes

Eye Contact Intelligence

Americans are firm in their belief that good eye contact is important during business and social conversations. In our country, direct eye contact is a sign of openness, honesty and assertiveness. Averting eye contact can be misconstrued as lack of confidence or deceptive. In many cultures, however, eye contact is avoided.

Consider the following guidelines:

- **South Korea** – Eye contact is important in business and at various other times. It ensures attention, shows sincerity, and forms a subtle but significant bond between individuals.

- **Middle East** – Eye contact is intense. Middle Easterners look intensely into a person's eyes to search their soul and evaluate their inner qualities. They look for dilated pupils to determine true interest in the people they are dealing with.

- **Thailand** – Eye contact is another form of communication by Thais. You can simply make brief eye contact with a waiter or waitress, and they will come to your table.

- **Scandinavia** – Eye contact is appreciated, but far less than that of Americans and British. Swedes look less frequently at their partners but hold their look for longer periods of time.

- **Mexico and Puerto Rico** – Direct eye contact is considered an aggressive gesture.

- **Japan** – Eye contact is considered slightly intimidating.

Gestures

Gestures are a casual, second-class form of communication, but people depend on these subtle movements, postures, actions and expressions as a shorthand. Like any other form of communication, gestures are culture-specific. A perfectly acceptable gesture in the U.S. may not be appropriate elsewhere.

For example, the "okay" gesture (made by connecting the thumb and fore-finger into a circle holding the other three fingers straight) in the U.S. is defined differently around the world:

- Japan – means money...looks like the shape of a coin.

- France, Belgium, Tunisia – worthless or zero.

- Brazil, Russia, Germany, Turkey, Greece, Malta – an orifice message.

- Throughout Europe – a vague, unspecific obscenity.

The "okay" sign is just one of millions of gestures that can turn a good day bad.

The selected examples highlight dramatically different cultures, attitudes, projection and demeanor traits. They should help give you a sense of how to research and "project" Cultural Awareness for future destinations. You should conduct more thorough research about the location where you will be traveling. The CIA World Fact Book is a great reference. Another good resource is Communicaid, a culture and communications skills consultancy with training centers in London, Paris, Frankfurt and New York offers country-specific data (www.communicaid.com).

"Why is it that traveling Americans are always so dreadful?"
—Dodsworth by Sinclair Lewis

Chapter 4 Review
Practice Assignment – Cultural Awareness

It's the Little Things That Count in Culture

In this chapter, we've explored how to blend in by studying and adapting to the local culture. Your advance preparation will be critical in determining the success of your trip.

Every culture has subtle differences. It's important to understand those nuances and not misinterpret them, or create misunderstandings by making an inadvertent mistake that is the result of ignorance. Let's take a look the challenges presented by a simple dinner invitation.

Practical Example

- Semi-permissive environment (area with some government control)

- Conducting sensitive business negotiations over dinner

You are in China on business and have tried to prepare carefully for these important meetings. In your pre-departure research, you learned that your most senior person should be your spokesperson for the introductory functions. You're a little frustrated with the pace of the meetings, but recognize that it is part of the Chinese culture to take business meetings slowly and to be very process-oriented. You are prepared for the agenda to become a jumping off point for other discussions. You've taken care to dress conservatively. If you are a man, you are wearing a dark-colored business suit. If you are a woman, you are wearing a conservative business suit or dress with a high neckline and flat shoes (or shoes with very low heels). You are avoiding bright colors.

You have been invited to dinner in the home of one of the Chinese business owners and are having trouble deciding what type of gift to bring for the hostess. You recognize this is an important gesture, and you're nervous about the local cultural protocol around gift-giving and dining.

Study Guide Questions

What sort of gift would be appropriate and what color gift-wrap should be avoided?

What should you do when you arrive and what sort of dining manners are important?

Study Guide Answers

What sort of gift would be appropriate and what color gift-wrap should be avoided?

Being invited to the home of a Chinese person is a great honor. The Chinese prefer to entertain in public places rather than in their homes, especially when entertaining foreigners. You should bring a small gift to the hostess.

In general, gifts are given at Chinese New Year, weddings, births and more recently (because of marketing) birthdays. The Chinese like food, so a nice food basket will make a great gift. Avoid gifts of scissors, knives or other cutting utensils as they indicate the severing of the relationship. Also avoid clocks, handkerchiefs or straw sandals as they are associated with funerals and death. Do not bring flowers, as many Chinese associate these with funerals. Do not wrap gifts in white, blue or black paper. Four is an unlucky number, so do not give four of anything. Eight is the luckiest number, so giving eight of something brings luck to the recipient. Always present gifts with two hands, and understand that gifts will not be opened when received. Gifts may also be refused three times before they are accepted.

What should you do when you arrive and what sort of dining manners are important?

Learn to use chopsticks, and be sure to arrive on time. Remove your shoes before entering the house, and wait to be told where to sit. The guest of honor will be given a seat facing the door. The host begins eating first and offers the first toast. Try everything that is offered to you, and never eat the last piece from the serving tray. Be observant of the needs of others. Return chopsticks to rest after every few bites and when you drink or stop to speak. Do not put bones in your bowl. Place them on the table or in a special bowl reserved for that purpose. Hold the rice bowl close to your mouth while eating. Do not be offended if a Chinese person makes slurping or belching sounds—these merely indicate enjoyment of the food. There are no strict rules about finishing all the food in your bowl, but eat well to demonstrate that you are enjoying the meal.

NOTES:

References Chapter 4

Business Travel Abroad, Department of State, Overseas Security Council, Diplomatic Publications, Released 1994.

Burton, Fred. Stewart, Scott. Threats, Situational Awareness and Perspective, Terrorism Intelligence Report, August 2007.

The CIA World Factbook www.cia.gov.

Eyring, Pamela. The Protocol School of Washington Curriculum, Washington D.C., 2008.

Communicaid www.communicaid.com.

Chapter 5

Third-Party Awareness

Determining Third-Party Awareness through Travelcraft

*"When you travel, remember that a foreign country
is not designed to make you comfortable.
It is designed to make its own people comfortable."*
—Clifton Fadiman

Third Party Awareness (3PA) is the general public's perception of you and your actions. By third parties, I mean citizens of the country in which you are traveling, law enforcement, criminals, or even a terrorist residing in or visiting the host country. As mentioned in Chapter 1, you cannot totally control the perceptions and judgments of others. To reduce Third Party Awareness, you need to blend into the environment using your Personal Awareness (the image and demeanor you project) and Situational Awareness skill sets.

If your Personal Awareness is high and you are in Alert Mode, then you already have partial control over Third Party Awareness. Increased Personal Awareness plus increased Situational Awareness equals decreased Third Party Awareness.

Travelcraft

You can determine who is scrutinizing you and your every movement through the use of *travelcraft™ techniques*. A travelcraft repertoire is a set of techniques that will help you assess whether you are under physical or technical surveillance. The spy world would call this tradecraft. Just to be clear, you don't want the wolf to think you're a spy. Trust me, you don't want the kind of attention that would result. The techniques you'll be using are non-alerting, allowing you to decrease your footprint without tipping anyone off to the fact that you think something is amiss. They are not designed to "bust" the bad guy or alert the surveillance team, but to increase your awareness, make you more confident as you transition through your Modes of Awareness cycle, and enable you to escape the wolf in a discreet manner.

The first phase of any criminal or terror attack is information collection. The bad guys want to know where you are staying, where you work, your modes of transportation, the routes you walk and drive, where you dine, and who you dine with. They want to know everything, in short, and all of this information will be used to determine your "pattern of life," a study of your daily, weekly and monthly activities. Once your "pattern of life" is analyzed, the crook or terrorist determines the vulnerabilities that set you up for attack, exploitation and kidnapping scenarios.

The first weapon in their arsenal is your routine, and your first line of defense is varying or shifting that routine. If your routine is always changing, it will keep potential threats off balance and make it difficult to target you. Break down your routines into three dimensions— time, routes and destinations. These must all be altered on a regular basis. The times you travel, the routes you walk or drive, and the places you go will determine their attack points. Constant changes make targeting difficult.

Timelines, routes and destinations are collected by both technical and physical surveillance. Which means that before we discuss defensive and detection techniques, you must gain a broad understanding of surveillance.

The subject of surveillance is extremely important to anyone conducting business abroad, as a traveler could be under surveillance for any number of reasons. Monitoring doesn't necessarily need to be conducted by foreign intelligence or a security service. Terrorists and criminals also use surveillance to plan their attacks. It should be noted that the risk is very low for the normal business traveler, who only spends a few days in each city and displays the proper projection and demeanor, to become a target for terrorists. The real terrorist threat to a traveler is being in the wrong place at the wrong time and becoming an inadvertent victim of a terrorist act. However, your risk for a criminal attack or an act of corporate espionage is much higher.

Surveillance is an assessment of vulnerabilities in an attempt to determine any information available, from any source, about you or your activities that can be used against you. If you recognize that you are under surveillance, then you can take preventive measures that will hopefully deter further interest. You won't be able to determine whether the surveillants are intelligence agents or terrorists, so you will need to be discreet in order to avoid tipping off those you suspect of watching you.

Surveillance takes many forms. An observer can be physically or electronically watching or monitoring your activities in your hotel room or office. Or you can be subject to mobile surveillance by being followed on foot or by a vehicle. *Physical Surveillance* consists of an individual or group of individuals physically following, observing and tracking every movement of a target. *Technical Surveillance* consists of following, observing and tracking a target with electronic equipment. Technical threats will be discussed in detail in Chapter 6.

Anatomy of Physical Surveillance

Active Surveillance (short-term): aggressive surveillance with an emphasis on actual 24/7 eyes-on surveillance. A trained surveillance team may employ this tactic pre-attack, pre-capture or pre-arrest. An untrained team may employ this technique and compromise themselves early due to overly aggressive tactics. Active surveillance consists of constant foot and mobile shadowing of the target by single or multiple surveillant(s) with hourly activity.

Passive Surveillance (long-term): loose, progressive surveillance with an emphasis on long-term, limited exposure to the target. A trained or untrained surveillance team may use this type of surveillance during an initial pattern of life analysis or when discretion is paramount. Passive surveillance would consist of *static* surveillance by single or multiple surveillant(s) staged at particular points of interest (e.g., home or work). Typically, no actual following of the target takes place.

Physical surveillance is an art, and it takes considerable amount of training for a team to be effective. For this reason, criminals or terrorist are considered sloppy and easy to spot. If you understand surveillance and use the Total Awareness system, amateur tactics will stand out. There are countless ways to conduct active and passive surveillance. I will briefly describe the most common.

Static Surveillance – Also known as *fixed surveillance*, this method consists of observing the target at a specific location from a fixed position. Static surveillance can be conducted from any location near or around the target person's residence, office or hotel.

Mobile Surveillance – Also known as *the follow*, this consists of observing the target while traveling or moving on foot and/or in a vehicle. Mobile surveillance collects information that cannot be collected by static surveillance.

Static and mobile surveillance can also be used concurrently to enhance the effectiveness of an operation.

Setting the Box: Most surveillance teams "pick up" a target from a static location like home or work. To "set the box," multimember, static surveillance teams cover all four sides of a structure. Each member covers possible exit and entrance points for the side of the structure used by the target person. A team member who observes the target departing or entering the structure will report a positive identification, location, dress and activity to the rest of the team.

Floating Box: Once the target moves from location to location, the surveillance team might employ a technique called a "floating box." The multimember mobile surveillance "box" will discreetly surround the target person during foot or mobile movement. Each member rotates in and out of position to maintain constant observation. This technique is very difficult for a team to perfect and employ. Risk of compromise is high.

Daisy Chain: A daisy chain can be used instead of a floating box to decrease possible compromise. A passive and static multimember linear surveillance model, it involves individual surveillants staged along a target's known route. The surveillants are typically ahead of the target, observing and reporting the target's arrival and departure at specific locations along the route.

These are just a few of the tactics that could be employed against you during your travels.

Physical Surveillance Recognition

As mentioned, almost every criminal act, from a purse snatching to a terrorist bombing, involves some degree of pre-operational surveillance. Criminals are vulnerable to detection during this time. Why? Because criminals, even militants planning terrorist attacks, often become quite sloppy when they are casing their intended targets. They have been able to get away with their careless tactics for so long because, sheep-like, most people simply do not pay attention. On a positive note, these shoddy practices will stand out to the totally aware sheepdog.

There are several ways to confirm surveillance, one of which goes by the acronym TEDD, for *Time, Environment, Distance* and *Demeanor*. In other words, surveillance can be assumed if you see someone repeatedly over *time*, in different *environments* and over *distance*; a conspicuous display of poor *demeanor* is another sign that you might be under surveillance.

By poor demeanor, I mean that a person is *acting* unnaturally. This behavior can look blatantly suspicious. It might be look like a person who is lurking around or has no reason for being where he is or for doing what he is doing. Sometimes, however, poor demeanor can be subtler. It can encompass almost imperceptible behaviors that the target senses more than observes. Other giveaways include moving when the target moves, communicating when the target moves, avoiding eye contact with the target, making sudden turns or stops, or even using hand signals to communicate with other members of a surveillance team.

In the terrorism realm, exhibiting poor projection can also include wearing unseasonably warm clothing, such as trench coats in the summer; displaying odd bulges under clothing or wires protruding from clothing; unnaturally sweating, mumbling or fidgeting; or attempting to avoid security personnel. In addition, according to some reports, suicide bombers often exhibit an intense stare as they approach the final stages of their mission.

They seem to have tunnel vision, being able to focus only on their intended target.

If you are a specific target of a planned attack, you may be able to use time, environment and distance to track TEDD, but if the subway car you are riding in or the building where you work is the target, you might only have the element of demeanor to key on. This is also true in the case of criminals who behave like "ambush predators" and lurk in an area waiting for a victim. Because their attack cycle is extremely condensed, the most important element to watch for is demeanor. Are you sick of hearing how important demeanor is yet?

Using the Modes of Awareness cycle will enhance your overall awareness to odd behaviors, unnatural posturing and suspicious acts. TEDD will enhance the decision and action arm of the OODA loop cycle, for it can be used not only to confirm surveillance but also to identify general criminal threats. There is, however, no single technique that can confirm or deny surveillance. Knowing the environment prior to departure, understanding the threats within the environment, and employing a Total Awareness approach at all times will insure that you have a good chance of detecting surveillance and its eventual consequences.

How to Confirm that You Are Under Physical Surveillance

Targeting

If you are traveling abroad on business, you could be targeted by an intelligence agency, a security service, or for that matter, a competitor, should you have knowledge of or be carrying sensitive or proprietary information. Certain indicators or situations are red flags, signaling unwarranted interest in your activities. These situations should be closely scrutinized and avoided, if at all possible. A few of the most common scenarios used by intelligence/security services, all of which have resulted in successful acquisition of information from the targeted individual, are listed below:

- Repeated contact with a local or third-country national who is not involved in your business interests or the purpose of your visit, but appears at each function as a result of invitations to social or business functions. This individual's demeanor may indicate more than just a passing interest in you and your business activities.

- A close relationship with a foreign national of a hostile host government is often unavoidable for business reasons. In these instances, be cautious and do not allow the relationship to develop any further than at a strictly business level.

- Be suspicious of an accidental encounter with an unknown local national who strikes up a conversation and wants to:

    - Practice English or other language.

    - Talk about your country of origin or your employment.

    - Buy you a drink because he or she has taken a liking to you.

    - Talk to you about politics.

    - Use a myriad of other excuses to begin a "friendly" relationship.

- If any of the above or anything else occurs that just does not ring true, BE SUSPICIOUS!! Such a scenario may be innocent, but it won't hurt to exercise prudence and good judgment.

- If you have any reason to believe that you are being targeted by an intelligence or security service or terrorist group, there is only one course of action to follow. Report your suspicions to the affiliate, embassy or consulate, and follow their guidance.

Anatomy of Technical Surveillance

Technical Surveillance is the following, observing and tracking of a target using electronic equipment. Chapter 5 will cover a myriad of technical threats. Here, I will discuss specific indicators that help you determine if technical monitoring equipment has been installed. The success of audio technical surveillance depends directly on human failure. So, I want to discuss the importance of communication security. Let face it, if you were able to keep your mouth shut, then concealed audio devices wouldn't be a threat. Big mouths coupled with big egos lead to nothing but big trouble. Here is an example.

In a live broadcast from the Iraqi desert, journalist Geraldo Rivera instructed his photographer to tilt the camera down to the sand in front of his feet so that he could draw a map. Rivera then outlined a map of Iraq and showed the relative location of Baghdad and his location with the Army's 101st Airborne unit. The reporter then continued with his diagram to illustrate where the 101st would be going next. Big news for everyone back home, but compromising of the operation he was with, the war, and the lives of soldiers. This very extreme example highlights how valuable information can be when delivered with little or no discretion.

As stressed, personal awareness is key to successfully eluding technical hits. Your projection and demeanor must remain consistent with your surroundings. Once again, if you're being watched, give them nothing to look for. If you're being listened to, give them nothing to hear. If you're being followed, give them nothing to see.

"Loose Lips Sink Ships"

Millions volunteered or were drafted for military duty during World War II. The majority of these citizen-soldiers had no idea how to conduct themselves to prevent inadvertent disclosure of important information to the enemy. To remedy this, the government established rules of conduct. The following is excerpted from a document given to each soldier as he entered the battle area.

COMSEC: Communication Security is a process by which a group or individual can deny adversaries information about intentions by identifying, controlling and protecting evidence of the planning and execution of travel.

1. Don't write military information of Army units—their location, strength, materiel or equipment.

2. Don't write of military installations.

3. Don't write of transportation facilities.

4. Don't write of convoys, their routes, ports (including ports of embarkation and disembarkation), time en route, naval protection, or war incidents occurring en route.

5. Don't disclose movements of ships, naval or merchant, troops, or aircraft.

6. Don't mention plans and forecasts or orders for future operations, whether known or just your guess.

7. Don't write about the effect of enemy operations.

8. Don't tell of any casualty until released by proper authority (the Adjutant General) and then only by using the full name of the casualty.

9. Don't attempt to formulate or use a code system, cipher, or shorthand, or any other means to conceal the true meaning of your letter. Violations of this regulation will result in severe punishment.

10. Don't give your location in any way except as authorized by proper authority. Be sure nothing you write about discloses a more specific location than the one authorized.

During World War II, all they had to worry about were handwritten blunders. Today, with technology-driven communication, these same blunders can be made via multiple mediums. Emails, phone conversations, texting, chat rooms, and more are areas of vulnerability. *Discipline and discretion are instrumental in preventing communication compromise.*

Technical Surveillance Recognition

On a positive note, most technical surveillance mechanisms require some kind of installation. Installation requires humans, humans with limited time whose stress responses can cause notable mistakes. Signs of these mistakes can indicate possible technical attacks within your hotel room, rental car or office space. Fortunately, with some work on your part, you may be able to detect these signs.

Intrusion Detection

Intrusion detection techniques—also known as traps, personal countermeasures or physical counter-measures—have been around for centuries, ever since sailors and pirates used thief knots (which look exactly like square knots) to tie up and secure their personal ditty bags. The intrusion detection technique was the knot itself. If a curious or thieving sailor or pirate were to open the ditty bag to view its contents without paying attention to the knot, they would naturally tie a square knot upon closure of the bag. Although the knots look similar, they are in fact very different. With that simple measure, the owner of the ditty bag would know that someone had been invading his privacy.

It's important that any intrusion detection technique you use be as natural and easy to remember as the thief knot. You do not want to set obvious traps, which may bring on even more scrutiny by the invaders. Intrusion detection techniques are meant to alert you to possible entry, not to bust the bad guy. There is no right or wrong technique as long as it's creative, natural to the environment, discreet and easy to remember, but here are two methods to consider. You should employ these "traps" in areas of concern.

Cardinal Bearings: You can set anything in a room or vehicle on a north, east, south or west alignment. For example, set a bottle of water near the USB ports of your laptop in your hotel room, and point any letter on the label of the water bottle "north." If the label is not aligned upon your return, you can assume attack. Similarly, you can hang the "do not disturb" sign on your doorknob so that a disruption of cardinal alignment betrays any unauthorized room entry—never fall prey to the assumption that a "do not disturb" sign will truly keep maids or other hotel employees out.

Discreet Alignment: Discreet alignment is the alignment of any object that has the potential for scrutiny or exploitation (e.g., a laptop, briefcase, documents and luggage) with another object or part of the room. For example, you could place a closed folder of documents on a desk and align or point the right corner at the alarm clock on the nightstand. Once again, if the corner of the folder is not pointed at the alarm clock upon your return, then it is safe to assume intrusion.

These techniques are limited only by your imagination and the environment. They can be used in your hotel room, office and rental car.

Technology can help determine if someone has intruded upon your personal space. The **Escape the Wolf Photo Trap** app, available for iPhone and Android, automatically compare before and after photos to detect the slightest differences in an environment. Detect footprints in grass, verify hard drive screws haven't been removed and reset, make sure no one has been rummaging through your drawers.

Hotel Rooms

Always assume that host nation government agencies have access to your room and are perfectly capable of conducting a room "toss," or search, if they so desire. An overt search will result in noticeable physical movement of items in the room. But a properly conducted covert search leaves no signs that a search took place at all. Government agencies will tend to have management open doors for them rather than break in clandestinely, which means that they will leave no signs of forced entry in their stead. Criminals or terrorists will not have the same luxury and will often leave behind tell-tale signs of a clandestine break-in. In either case, however, signs of a covert search can be detected via a series of careful checks and balances.

Upon entering the hotel room for the first time, take a mental snapshot of the room. Set a mental baseline by noting the following:

- the general condition of the door, door jam and door surface

- the floor directly under and around power outlets, phone outlets, air vents and other electronics (common technical installation points)

- how clean or dirty those areas are and any displacement of the carpet in and around those areas

- whether the windows are locked or unlocked and whether access points from balconies, ladders or other vantage points could be used to enter your room

- the cleanliness of the windowsills

Remember, the room may have already been "hit," so don't do anything that would alert anyone who might be monitoring you. This checklist can be performed on an initial walk-through of the hotel room, while retaining a relaxed, discreet manner.

Once you've set your mental baseline, it will be much easier to notice any changes or discrepancies. Each time you re-enter the room, note any changes—scarring or chipped paint in and around the door-locking mechanisms, door jam and strike plates. Note any additional sheetrock particles, dust, paint chips, wiring, or other signs of installation in and around power outlets, phone outlets, air vents and other electronics within the room. By paying attention and using intrusion detection techniques, you will enhance your ability to detect possible technical attacks. In any case, good projection and demeanor will prove the installs worthless to those trying to collect information about you or your company.

Rental Cars

Rental cars are no different than hotel rooms—except for the fact that a rental car is actually more likely to be "hit" than a hotel room. All in all, vehicles are easy targets for technical attacks. They are easy to break into—and due to their small size, easy to bug with a quick installation. They have built-in batteries that can power installed devices. They are usually left alone all night, and they are prime places for mobile phone conversations. (Most people feel comfortable talk about anything once "safely" inside a vehicle.)

Fortunately, personal awareness can eliminate this threat completely. Here are some tips to help you identify technical monitoring installations in a vehicle:

- Keep rental vehicles soiled. Note the displacement patterns of dirt around windows and doors. This will make it easier to identify possible entry. It's hard for bad guys to replace dust and dirt and make it look natural.

- Pay attention to pre-existing soiled areas on the hood and its margins. The soiled areas could be cleaned along with the bad guy's fingerprints.

- With clean vehicles, pay attention to existing smudge marks, handprints and weather stripping.

- Pay particular attention to the passenger side of a vehicle. A trained entry specialist will always enter through entry points opposite of driver.

- Removal of floor mats makes cleanup more difficult for the bad guy. His droppings cannot be simply dumped from the floor mat into a bag. He will actually have to pick debris off the floor and out of the carpet.

- Examine the interior dash, stereo, air conditioning, and accessory plastic housings and moldings for scars, scratches and misalignment. Removal of plastic parts with metal screwdrivers can leave scars behind.

- Look for wire, wire insulation, metal filings and plastic filings on floorboards, floor mats and outside entry points.

- As for your parking choice: the more public, the better.

Other Technical Ruses

A surveillance team can introduce a technical device by means of a "Trojan Horse," a technique coined in honor of the way the Greeks famously gained entry to the city of Troy during the Trojan War by building a massive, hollow wooden horse and hiding a group of elite Greek soldiers inside. The Greeks delivered the horse to the front gate of Troy and pretended to sail away. Thinking the horse an admission of defeat and a gift to the victors by the Greeks, the Trojans pulled the giant wooden horse within the city walls and celebrated their triumph. Unknowingly, they had just invited the Greek soldiers inside the city.

Ever since, the "Trojan Horse" has been a valued trick used by many people, groups and governments over time. Today, a technical device delivered right to your hotel room can work in much the same manner, so beware of random deliveries of welcome gifts, promotional items and any other products that could conceal a technical device.

One surprisingly common technique is to leave a removable computer USB flash drive on the ground of a company parking lot. An employee innocently comes along and thinks they've scored a free flash drive. They pop it into their computer, and the device silently steals company data and sends back a signal to an offsite thief.

Along those same lines, a technical device can be installed on items that you must check or store for short periods of time. For example, if you go to a restaurant and check your coat, a device could be installed while you dine. If you allow a hotel bellboy to take your luggage to your room, your luggage could be vulnerable to technical hits. These kinds of methods are virtually unlimited, so always be suspicious of Trojan horse installations, and never let anything important leave your sight.

Anti-Surveillance or "Escape"

Anti-surveillance measures consist of actions taken to elude or escape a possible surveillance team. You can employ anti-surveillance techniques regardless of whether surveillance is actually detected. If you are like me and assume you are being followed at all times, anti-surveillance may be the tool of choice. How you employ it is the important part. The goal is to successfully employ it without the surveillance team realizing it. An easy way to do so is to set up the surveillance team for failure from the very beginning.

One anti-surveillance tactic is the creation of an "accordion effect" that spreads out the surveillance team beyond recovery and forces them to lose sight of you. An easy way to do this is by driving from congested areas to non-congested areas and back. For example, driving through a downtown environment with lots of traffic lights, jumping onto a highway, and then exiting into another congested area will naturally cause the surveillance to get stretched out. One rule that surveillance teams know is that "density determines distance." If a team gets into a dense or congested area, they will tactically close up the distance between themselves and their target; in a rural area, the team will increase the distance between themselves and the target. By going back and forth between the two environments, you will essentially use this rule against them. Ultimately, creativity always wins, whether you're the target or the surveillance team. Just make sure you're always more creative than the adversary.

Most anti-surveillance tactics can be used on foot, but will be more difficult to perform discreetly. In a car, you can speed up and slow down, use your mirrors, and go varying distances from point to point. When you're on foot, you can't start running, constantly looking back, or hiding in the bushes—unless you want to really elevate Third Party Awareness. What you *can* do is use public transportation, congested shopping malls, and multilevel buildings to lose surveillance. Getting "lost" in density is a great way to make the surveillance team think that they lost you, versus thinking that you losing them. Anti-surveillance tactics are endless, but employing them properly and discreetly is the difficult part. Just remember: If you get caught, you better have your story straight.

The "X" Factor – Understanding the Ambush

If you use the Total Awareness system, getting caught is preventable, but as mentioned, no system is 100 percent foolproof. There are, however, some tactics and techniques you can use to escape if someone tries to capture you. The first, and simplest, is to sidestep the threat of capture by avoiding what I call the "X" factor.

The "X" is an invisible zone where your adversary or attacker might decide to ambush you with speed, stealth, and most certainly, surprise. Your attacker determines the location along your route where you are most vulnerable or distracted and then strikes with lightning speed, hoping to catch you totally unaware. The chosen location provides the attacker the greatest possibility of success with the least amount of attention from third parties. Remember, most bad guys don't want to get caught, so that limits their option to Xs that are not surrounded by curious bystanders, law enforcement or witnesses. The X can be an area where you are driving, walking, sitting or working.

The X doesn't have to be a particular spot on the ground. Remember the attempted action against me in Tanzania? The X was somewhere between the motorcycle-borne surveillant and the two cars pretending to be broken down. Potential ambush scenarios aren't like a Roadrunner and Coyote cartoon. There's no big block letter "X" marking the spot where the Coyote intends to roll the boulder down on the Roadrunner.

The chosen X, wherever it is, provides the attacker with three distinct advantages over you — *speed, stealth* and *surprise.*

> *Speed.* Logistically speaking, speed allows the attacker to capture or kill you and disappear with minimal time on the X.

> *Stealth.* The chosen X provides the attacker with cover and concealment points where he can remain invisible until the attack.

> *Surprise.* The chosen X provides the attacker the greatest opportunity to catch you off guard and minimizes your ability to respond against an attack.

Just knowing these three elements provides you with a huge advantage. As you use your Modes of Awareness cycle more often, you will start to identify possible Xs. Once you start identifying Xs, mentally running through reaction scenarios will better prepare you for a possible attack. Practicing this over time will ultimately put you ahead of any adversary, no matter how much preparation he puts into his attack. To get you ready, let's first dig into the anatomy of an ambush.

The Ambush

The ambush is a long-established military tactic in which the attacker uses concealment to attack a moving or stationary target. Ambushes have consistently been used in warfare throughout history, but have also been adopted by petty thieves, kidnappers and terrorists. Attackers strike from concealed positions within dense underbrush, behind hilltops, behind buildings, and around any corner or alley in the world. As mentioned, there are three fundamental parts to an ambush to ensure success — *speed, stealth* and *surprise.*

Speed. The attacker doesn't want to spend any more time than necessary in or around the X. The attacker wants the action against you to be quick and effective, leaving little time for reaction. The attacker wants to maintain a plan or schedule of events. The planned action is going to be executed as fast as possible in order to prevent detection, decrease reaction time by you and third parties. Bottom-line, time is very valuable to the attacker. Why is this important to us? We can take advantage of the attacker's need for speed. If we increase our speed, then we decrease the effectiveness of the attacker's plan. Moving fast through possible Xs and moving fast while under attack will greatly handicap the attacker's plan.

Stealth. The attacker needs the ability to hide or conceal himself until the right moment. His concealment must be invisible to you and not look suspicious to third parties. Concealment points must provide the ability to observe you without detection while providing easy access to you during the attack. There are a lot of variables to being stealthy that limit the options of attack. Why is this important to us? If we know the attacker must hide from us, yet still observe us and have access to us for the attack, we have a better sense of where to look for him and identify him prior to attack. The Modes of Awareness cycle will help you sift through possible Xs and concealment locations.

Surprise. The attacker wants to catch you completely off guard and paralyze you. He wants to dominate without a fight and strike fear in you with violence of action so there is little or no response from you. It's important to acknowledge surprise and rehearse it in your mind. Running mental "what if" scenarios with possible courses of action will help to diffuse the element of surprise when it occurs. You can use your Modes of Awareness cycle to factor in the element of surprise and move from Alert Mode to Crisis Mode. Then, use your OODA loop to transition back to Pre-Crisis. Having this system in place will increase survivability exponentially.

The goal within any human-versus-human encounter is to prevail and survive. As mentioned in prior chapters, you want to limit exposure to the threat and increase survivability. To do this, you must have the proper mental tools (Modes of Awareness cycle), tactics (travelcraft techniques) and skill (constant use of both).

Practical Example

Consider this simple scenario. You are walking down a super scary alley at night and confronted by a bum hiding behind a trashcan. The bum is focused only on you and begins the attack (action). Whether he knows it or not, the bum is using an OODA loop and is fixated on you with blinding tunnel vision and a surge of adrenalin. Once *your* OODA loop begins, you *Observe* the threat, you *Orient* to the threat, you make a *Decision* and then you *Act* (the reaction).

You quickly switch from Alert Mode to Crisis Mode by stepping laterally to the left or the right. At this point you should dodge his attack and then sprint away from the X. By moving off the X and out of the focus of the adrenalin-hyped, locked-on bum, you have caused him to readjust to you. You have now gotten inside of the bum's OODA loop. More importantly, it is much harder to hit a moving target than a stationary one.

Bottom line. GET OFF THE X AS SOON AS POSSIBLE!

Okay, now let's talk worst-case scenario. Your Modes of Awareness cycle has failed you. You have been caught off guard and are standing smack center on the X. Before you know it, you are taped up, blindfolded, and have found yourself in the trunk of a car.

Let's rewind and make some important points. First, and foremost, fight, fight, fight! Increase the time on the X by struggling, and you will decrease the attacker's speed and timeline.

Scream and yell like a banshee, minimizing the attacker's stealth and increasing Third Party Awareness. You want people to see you being attacked. You want people to see your attackers, the car they are driving, and every other detail possible. Decrease the effectiveness of restraints by fighting as hard as you can and don't stop. Every opportunity to claw, crawl or run should be made. If after all that, you still find yourself trapped in the trunk of a moving car...

THE FIGHT IS NOT OVER!

Escape

There is a point of no return where you may have to stop fighting, keep your wits about you, and surrender temporarily. Some events that might force capitulation would be the barrel of a gun pressed against your head, being overpowered by several attackers, being tasered or stun-gunned or receiving several substantial blows to the head. Point being, you want to live, not die.

Even while you temporarily surrender, you should be transitioning between modes and using your OODA loop to survey the environment. Most people think there are only two options, rescue or death. Escape never crosses their minds. If you're prepared, you won't even think about rescue or death. You will be too busy making your way back home.

Two tools to carry at all time: a razor blade and handcuff key. You can hide these in a variety of locations. Just make sure you can retrieve either one while blindfolded with your hands and feet restrained. The best time to free yourself is situation-dependent. Usually, the sooner the better. Too much time in custody could lead to detailed searches, being stripped naked, or death.

Your goal is to escape from your captors, but first you're going to have to escape from your restraints. Straightjackets, handcuffs, leg irons, ropes, chains and tape are among the more common restraints. The most popular restraint used by criminals and terrorists alike is tape, specifically clear threaded packing. It's cheap, available worldwide and faster to use than rope, chains, handcuffs or zip ties. This is yet another piece of knowledge that is priceless. Research how to escape from tape and other restraints before you ended up getting all wrapped up in it. (The next section provides some tips.)

If you're being restrained, the good news is that someone wants you around for a while. You are alive and being given a chance to turn the tables on your captors. Work fast and keep your wits about you.

Become a Houdini

Like most kids, I was mystified by magic. While traveling with my family in Hong Kong, I was lured by street vendors selling close-up, sleight-of-hand magic tricks. The vendors would perform a trick and wouldn't reveal how it was done until the purchase of the trick. Before I knew it, I had 20-plus tricks. Thanks, Dad. Over time I became really good at close-up magic. Whether it was coins, spongy balls, playing cards or handkerchiefs, I was hooked. As with other types of magic, much of the intrigue raised the question, "How did you do that?" Of course, a magician never reveals the secret, nor does he do a trick twice.

There are some magic secrets worth revealing, however, because they have the power to save your life. Many come from the great magician Harry Houdini, who figured out the process of escape decades ago.

One of Houdini's rules of escape certainly applies to escaping the wolf. It is this: *Never attempt to perform an escape that you aren't certain you'll achieve.* This means that whether the restraint method is tape, rope, chain or cuffs, you must practice to be proficient. It also means that if the possibility of death starts to raise its ugly head, you must stop the fight and act accordingly in order to survive.

For Houdini, of course, escapes were about showmanship. Audiences would flock to see his performances, the real attraction being his persona and his *presentation*.

The takeaway for those of us engaged in an escape that *is* a matter of life and death is *presentation*. We're not talking about showmanship, however, but about how you present yourself to the wolf when he is taking you captive. The setup for a successful escape starts with this. In his 1921 book, *Magical Rope Ties and Escapes*, Houdini explained many of his strategies:

> "If the committee . . . begin to make more knots than suits you, it will be well to swell the muscles, expand the chest, slightly hunch the shoulders, and hold the arm a little away from the sides. After a little practice you will find that such artifices will enable you to

balk the most knowing ones. You should always wear a coat when submitting to this tie, as that will be found to be an added help in obtaining slack . . ."

By creating gaps and doing what I call "getting big" during capture, you create slack in the tape, rope or chains used to subdue you. This is the art of presentation. You want to make your chest as big as possible, keep your elbows away from your sides, and keep your wrists, knees and ankles apart. Remember, while on the X, the attackers want to move fast and limit their exposure to public attention. You've already worn them out with a fight and made lots of noise. Now, you are being overwhelmed by sheer numbers or gunpoint. Escape on the X is becoming less likely. So what do you do? GET BIG! The attackers will be tired and working fast. This is your best opportunity to set yourself up for a sooner-rather-than-later escape.

Houdini wasn't opposed to a little trickery, and you shouldn't be either:

> "A sharp knife with a hook-shaped blade should be concealed somewhere on the person, as it may be found useful in case some of the first, carefully tied knots prove troublesome. A short piece cut from the end of the rope will never be missed."

Houdini's amazing ability to escape from handcuffs led to his discovery by vaudeville impresario Martin Beck in 1899. Although Houdini was hardly the first or only performer to do handcuff escapes, he would take the act to a new level over the next several years. As the "Handcuff King," Houdini gained his first measure of fame. There was no one "secret" to Houdini's ability to escape from handcuffs, but rather a combination of technical knowledge, physical skill and trickery. Most of the time Houdini used a key hidden in or smuggled into the cabinet or jail cell, either pre-staged within his clothing or left earlier by an assistant. Depending on how he was bound, Houdini would manipulate the keys with his hands—sometimes using specially designed extension rods—or with his teeth.

Houdini also knew tricks for opening many of the simpler types of cuffs without keys. In *Handcuff Secrets*, a book he published in 1910 to discourage the legion of imitators trying to ride his coattails, Houdini wrote,

> "You can open the majority of the old-time cuffs with a shoestring. By simply making a loop in the string, you can lasso the end of the screw in the lock and yank the bolt back, and so open the cuff in as clean a manner as if opened with the original key."

As he demonstrated in his own defense during a German slander trial in 1902, some cuffs could be opened simply by being banged against a hard surface, which might include a lead plate fastened at the knee under his trousers.

Houdini also used tricks that didn't involve opening locks. If presented with a particularly difficult lock, he might insist it be placed higher on his forearm, and then simply slip these cuffs over his wrists.

The takeaway – It's not difficult to place pre-staged handcuff keys and razor blades within your clothing in positions that are easy to reach while tied up. Can't imagine you would carry these items? You might want to if you are traveling into a non-permissive environment or an area where there are a large number of kidnappings. There are many places where you can purchase such resources off the Internet. (Attendees of *Escape the Wolf* travel security awareness training programs receive these and other life-saving survival tools as part of their course materials.)

Don't be fooled, though. Removing handcuffs is an extremely difficult maneuver that takes a significant amount of practice.

Travelcraft skills are like playing chess. The move you make now sets you up for success later. Fortunately, the bad guys typically play checkers, and don't notice what your moves could tell them about the future.

So, sit facing the door. Pay for your meals first. Know that pepper and salt burn the eyes, and always know where the back door is located.

"Travel is more than the seeing of sights;
it is a change that goes on, deep and permanent,
in the ideas of living."
—Miriam Beard

Chapter 5 Review
Practice Assignment – Third Party Awareness

It's Tempting, but Don't Mess with Surveillance

This chapter has shown you how to determine if you are being targeted for surveillance. You've learned how to identify when your hotel room or car might have been tampered with and how to determine if technical surveillance equipment has been installed. Those are sobering possibilities, but they are possibilities you should take seriously. They may never happen to you, but it's better to be prepared. Let's take a look at a real-life example— an example of what you *shouldn't* do when under surveillance.

Practical Example

• Semi-permissive environment (area with some government control)

• Being followed by a surveillance team

When a host nation has limited surveillance resources, a lack of training, or just the desire to intimidate you and prevent you from getting work done, they may perform what is known as a "bumper lock." This tactic consists of obvious overt surveillance of you and your activities. In short, the surveillance team is always right behind you, in your rearview mirror, opening the supermarket door for you, there when you wake up, and tucking you in at night. Decision-making while under this kind of coverage is difficult.

Is it a government-sponsored surveillance team who thinks I am a spy? Is it a bunch of criminals who want to steal my rental car? Or are they a bunch of terrorists who want to chop my head off? You cannot positively determine who "they" are or what their intentions are, so what do you do? This is probably one of the most difficult equations. The answer resides within the person being followed. A true spy would tell you to embrace surveillance. Bore them. Get them to fall in love with you so that you can take advantage of them when it's time.

I experienced this situation when I landed in a former Eastern bloc country to survey possible threat vulnerabilities to a U.S. installation. I was immediately bumper locked from the airport to the hotel. In my rear view mirror, I could see a white Toyota Corolla with four large white males crammed inside. The chances were very high that they were government-sponsored surveillance just curious to see what I was doing and why I was there. I figured that because of lack of resources and training it was easier for them to just bumper lock and see what I would do, how I would react, and what my level of training was than to engage in covert surveillance. My job was to embrace them, act like I did not see them, and carry on with my job in a very boring, unappealing manner.

Even I got bored with this particular assignment and decided to have fun with my new friends. So, one day as I drove around town, doing nothing but shopping, eating and playing tourist, I decided to play with the team of goons. As you may or may not know, other less fortunate government agencies think that the United States has thousands of invisible Unmanned Airborne Vehicles (UAVs) soaring through the skies like eagles. They think these gunships are hovering on standby in every country ready to launch rockets at anything that moves, and that each American spy has a satellite issued to him or her like a pair of jungle boots. Obviously not true, but why not take advantage of this myth, just for fun?

At each of my stops, I would park, exit my rental car, look at my watch, and then look at the sky. The goons didn't notice at first. They would typically park and exit their Toyota. One would follow me into whatever establishment, and the others would hang out and smoke. By the second day and third stop, they must have noticed my strange habit of looking at my watch and then looking up at the sky. At the fourth stop, all goons stayed in their vehicle and rolled down the windows. Four heads popped out, peering up to the sky trying to see what I was looking at. I couldn't help but laugh (to myself of course).

At the end to the day, I returned to my hotel room, where I found all the contents of my luggage scattered neatly about my room, the furniture re-arranged, and my toilet filled with a fresh present. Touché!

Study Guide Questions

Should I have taunted the bad guys who had me under surveillance?

What would you have done in that situation?

Study Guide Answers

Should I have taunted the bad guys who had me under surveillance?

As tempting as it was, it's never wise to taunt surveillance, nor is it smart to reveal your skills or training. This gives a surveillance team a reason to tighten up on you. Also never assume that the surveillance is government-sponsored. You could be dealing with terrorists.

Keep in mind, a trained spy can usually use his training, experience, and other resources to determine the nature of surveillance. A businessperson lacks those skills but is equally vulnerable to surveillance. You could be followed by government agents who think you are a spy dressed like a businessperson, or that you have trade secrets that would benefit their economy. Remember, governments all over the world are committing time and resources to corporate espionage, hoping to obtain the latest information that could help their economy. But it could simply be bad guys wanting to take your Rolex.

Whatever the nature of the threat, it's imperative that you use your Modes of Awareness cycle to detect it. Always report surveillance to your corporate chief security officer (if you are a businessperson), the embassy, and the individual or entity you are doing business with, in that order. Your report to your company will be logged for that destination. The report to the embassy will be investigated through host nation contacts. Your report to whomever you're doing business with will let them know that you are smarter than the average bear. The more who know, the better, particularly if you should happen to suddenly disappear.

What would you have done in this situation?

When you think you're being followed, keep these things in mind:

- Never take surveillance lightly.

- Always remain calm.

- Always use your Modes of Awareness cycle. Don't get rearview mirror tunnel vision.

- Always keep surveillance happy.

- Exhibit good Personal Awareness. Always appear boring, unimportant and unappealing. They may decide to stop watching you and shift to someone more important (a non-*Escape the Wolf* reader).

- Practice good Situational Awareness. Always take note of the license plate number, vehicle make, model and color of the surveillance vehicle that is tracking you. If possible, remember the human characteristics for each surveillance team member, using the Dominant Identifying Characteristics chart in Chapter 2.

NOTES:

References Chapter 5

Ball, Kirstie. Lyon, David. Maurakami, David. Wood, Clive. Charles Raab, Norris. A Report on the Surveillance Society, For the Information Commissioner by the Surveillance Studies Network, September 2006.

Burton, Fred. Stewart, Scott. Threats, Situational Awareness and Perspective, Terrorism Intelligence Report, August 2007.

Business Travel Abroad, Department of State, Overseas Security Council, Diplomatic Publications, Released 1994.

Carjacking: Don't be a Victim, Overseas Security Advisory Council, Department of State, OSAC Publication 2005.

Counterterrorism, The National Counterterrorism Center, Counterterrorism Calendar, September 2008.

McCullagh, Decian. RFID Tags: Big Brother in Small Packages. CNET News. January 13, 2003.

Surveillance Countermeasures, ACM 4 Security Services, Paladin Press, Boulder Colorado. 1994.

Vlahos, James. Surveillance Society: New High-Tech Cameras Are Watching You. Popular Mechanics. January 2008.

Chapter 6

THREAT

The Wolf's Many Forms

"The traveler was active; he went strenuously in search of people, of adventure, of experience. The tourist is passive; he expects interesting things to happen to him. He goes 'sight-seeing.'"
—Daniel J. Boorstin

A key element in avoiding or escaping the wolf is understanding what the wolf looks like, researching where he operates, and determining the odds of running into him. Threats (or wolves) appear in many shapes and forms. In this chapter, I will discuss threats with a broad brush, identifying some of the more common threats and showing you how to deal with them. Because new threats are constantly emerging and every location has particularities of its own, the information in this chapter should be used only as a jumping-off point for your own, destination-specific research.

As simple as it may sound, threats are usually unknown adversaries, obstacles or situations that take you by surprise. Some threats are completely avoidable with proper preparation. Others can be countered by adapting to the situation with calm, educated reactions or decisions. A large number of threats can be neutralized through proper presentation, projection and demeanor. Of course, some threats are unavoidable and will take you by surprise no matter how prepared you are. By practicing good Personal Awareness and Situational Awareness, you can reduce those surprises dramatically.

For this discussion, THREAT is not only our topic, but also an acronym categorizing risks of a variety of natures—Technical, Health, Raids, Environment, Agencies, and Terrorism. The following broad definitions lay out common worldwide dangers in each of these categories.

Technological Threats: Technological threats include audio collection devices, video collection devices, tracking devices, and cell phone, tablet and laptop exploitation used to collect information illegally.

Health Threats: Health threats include viruses, bacteria, chemicals, and other harmful substances spread human-to-human, airborne-to-human, water or food-to-human, and vector-to-human. I will also cover some of the more popular disease processes, signs and symptoms, and treatment. Your research should also identify poisonous reptiles, insects and any other animals that could pose a threat in specific locations.

Raids/Robbery: These types of threats include organized assaults conducted by criminals or terrorists. By definition, a criminal is a person guilty of a crime or crimes. Criminals commit theft, rape, murder and everything in between. The most significant raids are kidnapping, carjacking and hostage situations.

Environmental Threats: Environmental threats include natural events like hurricanes, tsunamis, winter storms, volcano eruptions and mudslides. I will discuss some types of disasters and actions to be taken. You will need to research specifics related to the area you plan to visit.

Agencies: Certain intelligence and law enforcement agencies are devoted to collecting information related to host government security and defense. I will identify and discuss different agencies, their intentions, and how they might affect you. Again, you will need to research specifics related to the area you plan to visit.

Terrorism: A terrorist is a person or group using unlawful acts of violence to influence, coerce, or create fear for ideological, political or religious gains. Currently, there is not an internationally agreed upon definition of terrorism. We will look at terrorist facts, groups and tactics. Again, you will need to look up specifics about active groups related to the area you plan to visit.

Before I discuss each of the threats, I want to stress once again the importance of embarking on country studies before you depart for your trip. It's important to develop the "shell" of a plan before you even set foot outside your home. Perhaps you've heard of the "Seven Ps" – "Proper Prior Planning Prevents Piss Poor Performance." There's a reason this saying has such resonance.

Take the time to research possible threats ahead of time. Start by writing THREAT vertically on a sheet of paper. Look up your country online. Then, begin filling in the blanks. Open source information is available on a number of great government websites.

Technical Threats

It was only about 60 years ago that the first computer was developed. It filled an entire room. Today, technology is micro in size and giant in capability, with a price tag even the poorest wolf can afford. Even in the farthest corners of the earth, you'll find Internet cafes filled with people surfing the web, emailing and socializing. But what are they really up to?

Methods of Collection

The world's most common methods of collection all involve photo, video, audio and tracking devices. Any of these devices could be implemented against you, whether overtly or covertly. Manned or unmanned, technologies can be used right out of the box and concealed in just about anything.

Photo and Video

Cameras are everywhere these days. I've read that in the United States you are filmed or photographed 50 to 75 times a day, and that number is growing. It doesn't take a rocket scientist to understand how that is possible, given all the cameras we encounter over the course of a given day via mobile device or at traffic stops, ATM machines, stores, restaurants, gas stations and more.

In other countries, like England, an individual has his or her image taken an average of 400 times a day. British intelligence can literally track a person who stays in London from the time of arrival at the airport to the time of departure. All cameras are synced together and "hand off" targeted individuals from camera to camera intuitively. England has over 300,000 cameras. There are 100 million in China. Are you paranoid yet?

Who Would Take Your Picture?

Individuals and entities who might be taking your photo when you are traveling include host nation law enforcement officials, intelligence agencies, members of the military, public transportation agencies, private security forces, shopping mall security and traffic-related systems. But here is a dose of reality: None of these agencies employ enough people to observe every camera feed in real time. Though most of these systems are on all the time and recording, they are reviewed only in the event of a crisis.

Who Uses Concealed Cameras?

Any of the above entities could use concealed cameras. Shopping districts use concealed cameras to watch the cash register, stored inventory, entrances and exits. China has installed cameras in cinemas and supermarkets. Host nation intelligence agents, terrorists and criminals alike will take an interest in you if you match a certain profile or if your demeanor says, "Look at me, I am a bad news American." Whatever you do, don't search your hotel room and rental cars for hidden cameras. If "they" are watching, then you just compromised yourself by visibly searching for signs of surveillance. Assume your hotel and rental car have either passive or active concealed cameras and act accordingly.

Countering Image Capture

The first step in countering image capture is to assume that your picture is being taken at every minute of the day and night. Through proper Total Awareness techniques, specifically projection and demeanor, you will give observers nothing to note. When in Alert Mode, you observe the cameras, orientate yourself accordingly, decide upon alternate routes, and take action to avoid future cameras. But the reality is that for every camera you spot, there are dozens you don't.

A proper demeanor reveals nothing to the people on the opposite side of those cameras. Depending on your occupation and reason for being in country, you may decide to use a light disguise, take advantage of lighting, or stress the limitations of the cameras you encounter. A light disguise consists of umbrellas, hats, sunglasses, and other accessories that could make identification difficult. Please keep in mind: if the attire isn't common within a particular culture, wearing it may bring more attention to you. Americans are the only ones who wear sunglasses religiously. Very few people overseas wear baseball-style caps except Americans. If you wear both, consider yourself targeted.

With or without accessories, you can use the sun or other light sources to your advantage. Putting yourself between the camera and a light source will effectively backlight you and make any image useless. Stressing the limitations of the camera's field of view and focal length can work to your advantage. For example, cash machine (ATM) cameras are angled and set to focus on face-size objects 8 to 12 inches away. Passing these machines within a distance greater than 12 inches will effectively result in a blurry image of you or your vehicle.

Audio Devices

Once again, any of the above entities may want to hear what you have to say. Depending on why you are in country, intelligence agencies, law enforcement, terrorist, and criminals may want a piece of your information. Information is what creates action, whether against you or others. It could be as innocent as where you'll be meeting your party for dinner. How is audio information collected? The most popular listening devices are ears. You never know who is listening, and if you have the gift of gab, assume someone will hear you. Remember Third Party Awareness and Communication Security from Chapter 5? This would be a good time to review it. Ultimately, good Personal Awareness, specifically demeanor (actions), will prevent this kind of collection.

The next most prevalent audio collection device is the mobile phone. There are programs that can be downloaded to a cell phone that allow a user to turn on another person's cell phone microphone without its owner knowing it. This allows them to use the targeted phone as a real-time listening device. These programs were developed for parents wanting to listen to their teenagers, but can be used against you just the same. Some host nation governments have systems that listen to all cell phone conversations originating in their country. Mobile phones are the single biggest communication platform—and also the single biggest technical surveillance threat.

Countering Mobile Phone Exploitation

The easiest countermeasure is to never use a mobile phone to begin with. Next best technique? Leave the phone outside your conversation zone. If you must have a phone on your person, turn it off and remove the battery. No battery, no power, no exploitation. Off is not good enough, because a phone that appears to be off can still be used as a listening device. Always remove the battery from your cell phone when discussing sensitive information while traveling. Don't switch out SIM cards, thinking you're being sneaky. That will only single you out all the more. Lastly, anything "made in China," especially technology should be considered bugged as a matter of course.

Concealed Audio Devices

Concealable audio devices can be employed just about anywhere, and if installed correctly, will be undetectable. These "bugs" come in all shapes and sizes. They can be installed in your hotel room, rental cars, popular bars, office, home and even an embassy. Once again, act as if someone is always listening and you won't have a problem. Demeanor, demeanor, demeanor!

Countering Covert Audio Devices

As with any form of anti-surveillance measures, countermeasures against audio surveillance need to be discreet. Don't actively look for devices. If there is video, you just burned yourself. Don't think turning the TV on is going to help, either. Readily available software can cancel out background noise. The best measure of protection is to always, always, always assume someone is listening, especially in your hotel rooms and rental cars.

Tracking

Tracking via technical device can be accomplished in several ways. Let's start with your passport, which probably contains a radio frequency identification (RFID) card—every passport issued after October 2006 it outfitted with this little computer chip. These chips have 64 kilobytes of memory, which contain your date of birth, nationality, gender, place of birth, and your digital photograph. Basically, everything that's printed in your passport is also on the chip. Though this measure is meant to improve security, it means not only that your passport can be scanned covertly, with all your info collected by a criminal or terrorist, but that you can also be tracked. If enough electrons are pumped into the RFID remotely, the passport becomes a beacon. With the right receiver and software, your location can be identified. Now, it would take a very technologically advanced intelligence or law enforcement agency, but the threat is there.

Your mobile phone can be a tracking device as well. On or off, it can be tracked—so once again, the only way to be sure it's not being used against you is to take the battery out when you suspect you are being followed. The government of any country owns the cell phone towers with which your mobile phone communicates regularly. It doesn't take much to watch your movements.

Rental cars are typically tracked for inventory control, vehicle relocation (if stolen or abandoned), and emergencies. Most use a cell phone-based technology. Once again, assume you are being tracked regardless of environment.

Concealed Tracking Devices

These days, anyone can purchase tracking devices right off the Internet. Extremely user-friendly and cheap, they come in a variety of shapes and sizes. Some are credit card size, others look like a large thumb drive or black brick. Depending on the device, they can be tracked in real time by websites, special receivers and even mobile phones. Other devices have to be physically removed to view stored data on a computer. They can be installed deep into a compartment in a vehicle or slapped under the bumper. Once again, don't actively look for these items. You may be compromising yourself to third parties.

Countering Tracking Devices

Time to sum up your basic defense system against all of these various kinds of technical threats.

Remove your mobile phone battery. Leave your passport in a safe place or wrap it up in three layers of foil. Among other life-saving survival tools, attendees of *Escape the Wolf* travel security awareness training programs receive a Zero Trace™ Pouch, which blocks tracking devices, as part of their course materials. The patented Zero Trace pouch helps prevent identity fraud, RFID collection, mobile phone exploitation and tracking. By placing all essential personal electronics and RFID latent credit cards, identification cards, access control cards and passports in the pouch, you gain a cloak of invisibility.

If you have to rent a vehicle, assume you're being tracked. Whenever possible, walk or use public transportation. If you're stuck with a rental and have sensitive business to conduct, park in underground parking garage. That will kill the signal of mobile phone and satellite-based tracking systems.

Laptop Security

Thinking of taking your laptop or tablet on the road? It's a great way to work and stay in touch when traveling. Believe you're all set because you have a firewall, up-to-date antivirus software, a strong password and encrypted data? Not quite. Once again, it's about awareness and taking a few simple precautionary steps. Consider doing the following to keep your laptop safe—and in your possession—when on the road:

- Treat it like the mountain of cash (or information) it is.

- Get it out of the car. Don't leave it behind—ever.

- Keep it locked. Use a security cable and attach it to something immovable or really heavy and hard to move.

- In a hotel, try not to leave your laptop in your room. If you must leave the laptop, use a security cable and put up a "do not disturb" sign.

- Keep it off the floor, or at least between your feet.

- Keep passwords separate—not near your laptop or case.

- Don't leave it "for just a sec," no matter where you are. Don't trust anyone, even those nice people in the coffee shop.

- Pay attention in airports, especially at security checkpoints.

- Use bells and whistles. If you've got a laptop alarm, turn it on. Or consider a "lo-jack" device that can help locate a missing laptop when it's connected to the Internet.

- Report a missing laptop IMMEDIATELY. If it's stolen, report the theft to the local authorities. Report a business laptop disappearance immediately to your employer. If it's your personal laptop and you fear identity theft, visit the Federal Trade Commission's identity theft web page for instructions.

Data Protection

To make sure no unauthorized person logs on to your system or changes settings, set up a BIOS (basic input/output system) password. The following is an example, using a Dell computer (GX260 and GX270). The process is similar for other Windows-based computers.

1. To get in the BIOS setup, boot up the computer and press **F2**. (The option comes up on the upper left hand corner of the screen.)

2. Highlight System Security, then press **Enter**.

3. Highlight System Password, then press **Enter** and put in the password. Confirm the password.

4. The system password will change from "not enabled" to "enabled."

5. Repeat process for Setup Password. Setup Password will change from "not enabled" to "enabled".

6. Highlight password status. Press **Space bar** to change password status from "unlocked" to "locked."

7. Press **Esc** twice and then highlight **Save and Exit,** press **enter.**

For MAC or other operating system instructions, see www. onguardonline.gov. After you have completed the above steps, you will need to enter the appropriate password to enter the system BIOS or to start the computer.

Use WinZip

WinZip is a company that offers encryption products for Windows users who are increasingly use and share files in a wide variety of environments. With multiple cloud services, social media platforms and messaging services, user data is at greater risk from online threats and hacks. WinZip protects files through sophisticated encryption and an additional layer of security requiring you to set your own password. Deleted files can be truly destroyed with the "wipe" feature.

The encryption is AES based. AES, Advanced Encryption Standard, was developed as a result of a three-year government competition by the U.S. National Institute of Standards and Technology (NIST). Also known as Rijndael, this is the Federal Information Processing Standard. WinZip's encryption comes in different strengths 128-bit or 256-bit. The numbers refer to the size of the encryption key used to encrypt the data, or protective wall that is built around the data. The higher the number, the stronger the encryption and faster the time to encrypt or decrypt the file, usually not noticeable. WinZip's compression and encryption capabilities now allow users to share on social media without compromising security.

Be sure to create a really, really strong password. Data security depends on the strength of the encryption method and the strength of your password. Two major factors of password strength are the length of the password and character selection. Use a mix of numerical and alpha characters, including capital letters. Do not put in the names of your kids or your pets or other biographical information. Avoid any actual words. The longer the password, the better. Yes, it's a pain, but well worth it.

Web Browsing

Several web browsers offer security advantages at the time of this writing, including Google Chrome and Firefox, over Internet Explorer. It's critical to regularly check on all web browsers, software and operating systems that you use to make sure you have the most secure products. A website like Secunia, http://secunia.com, is a great resource and can email alerts on security issues.

Here are a few features offer by Foxfire, in addition to its anti-malware, anti-virus software, a pop-up blocker and anti-phishing protection, to guard against certain technical threats:

> **Instant Web Site ID** - By clicking on a website favicon, you can get an instant identity overview to confirm a site's legitimacy. Another click digs deeper: How many times have you visited? Are your passwords saved? Check on suspicious sites, avoid Web forgeries, and make sure a site is what it claims to be.

> **Private Browsing** – This feature, also available on Google Chrome, protects your browsing history and allows you to slip in and out of private browsing mode quickly. This is a useful application for checking email from an Internet café.

Forget This Site - Having second thoughts about having visited a certain Web site? This feature removes every trace of the site from your browser.

Outdated Plug-In Detection - Some web pages require that you install small applications called plug-ins to watch videos, play games or view documents. Since these plug-ins are written by other companies, it can be hard to make sure they're always up to date. Since outdated plug-ins are a security risk, Firefox lets you know when you have a plug-in that's vulnerable to attack and directs you to the right site to get the updated version.

Clear Recent History - Clear all your private data or just your activity over the past few hours with a few quick clicks. You have full control over what to delete, and then your info is gone for good— whether you're browsing on your own computer or the one at your local library.

Customized Security Settings – You can control the level of scrutiny you'd like Firefox to give a site. Customize settings for passwords, cookies, loading images and installing add-ons.

Password Manager – You can choose to remember site passwords without intrusive pop-ups. The "remember password" notification is integrated into your view at the top of the site page.

CCleaner

This software system optimizer, privacy and cleaning tool removes unused files from your system and allows Windows to run faster. It also cleans traces of your online activities.

To conclude, a very wise man, KB, once told me:

- *Someone can always see you; don't give them a reason to watch.*

- *Someone can always hear you; don't give them a reason to listen.*

- *Someone can always find you; don't give them a reason to look.*

Health Threats

Health threats are global and inescapable to a certain degree. You can wash your hands, burn your food, spray everything down with bleach, and still get sick. There are millions of diseases that hide throughout the globe. Some more common than others. In this section, I will cover diseases that I have obtained overseas or witnessed, or you may encounter more frequently. Once again, I cannot stress the importance of country studies prior to departure. With a country study, you can determine what diseases exist, in what seasons the diseases are more prevalent, what immunizations are required, and whether prophylaxis can be taken to combat them.

Beyond Diseases

You should also research other types of threats that may jeopardize your health, such as environmental conditions. These threats often aren't top of mind when preparing to travel.

Air Pollution has become a major health concern in many countries and regions of the world. Large cities such as Beijing, New Delhi, Mexico City and Cairo receive all the headlines, but many other less populated areas suffer from poor air quality due to geography, weather patterns and the high polluting industries found there. Symptoms include coughing, shortness of breath, wheezing, itchy watery eyes, chest pain, nausea and headaches.

Everyone is affected differently by air quality. As with everything else, do your research and understand what you will be encountering during your travels. A couple of valuable resources on worldwide air pollution are the World Health Organization and AirNow.gov.

Animals and Insects Out of more than 3,000 species of snakes in the world, some 600 are venomous. WHO has launched a website http://apps.who.int/bloodproducts/snakeantivenoms/database/ in an effort to decrease the estimated 100,000 deaths that occur from snake poison annually. The site contains a database of approved anti-venoms to treat the 2.5 million people who suffer venomous bites each year. In addition to poisonous snakebites, there are poisonous spider and insect bites. It's important to research all the various health hazards you might encounter in the areas you plan to visit.

Malaria

- Malaria is a life-threatening disease caused by parasites transmitted to people through bites of infected mosquitoes.

- A child dies of malaria every 30 seconds.

- There were 247 million cases of malaria in 2006, causing about 880,000 deaths, mostly among African children.

- Malaria is preventable and curable.

- Approximately half of the world's population is at risk of malaria, particularly those living in lower-income countries.

- Travelers from malaria-free areas to disease "hot spots" are especially vulnerable to the disease.

Malaria is caused by parasites of the species *Plasmodium*. The parasites are spread to people through the bites of infected mosquitoes.

Transmission

Malaria transmission rates can differ depending on local factors such as rainfall patterns (mosquitoes breed in wet conditions), the proximity of mosquito breeding sites to people, and types of mosquito species in the area. Some regions have a fairly constant number of cases throughout the year. These countries are termed "malaria endemic." In other areas, there are "malaria seasons," usually coinciding with the rainy season.

Large and devastating epidemics can occur when the mosquito-borne parasite is introduced into areas where people have had little prior contact with the infecting parasite and have little or no immunity to malaria, or when people with low immunity move into areas where malaria cases are constant. These epidemics can be triggered by wet weather conditions and further aggravated by floods or mass population movements driven by conflict.

Symptoms

The common first symptoms—fever, headache, chills and vomiting—usually appear 10 to 15 days after a person is infected. If not treated promptly with effective medicines, malaria can cause severe illness and is often fatal.

At Risk Populations

Most cases and deaths are in sub-Saharan Africa. Asia, Latin America, the Middle East and parts of Europe, however, are also affected. In 2006, malaria was present in 109 countries and territories.

- Travelers from malaria-free regions, with little or no immunity, who go to areas with high disease rates are very vulnerable.

- Non-immune pregnant women are at high risk of malaria. The illness can result in high rates of miscarriage and cause more than 10% of maternal deaths (soaring to a 50% death rate in cases of severe disease) annually.

- Semi-immune pregnant women risk severe anemia and impaired fetal growth even if they show no signs of acute disease. An estimated 200,000 of their infants die annually as a result of malaria infection during pregnancy.

- HIV-infected pregnant women are also at increased risk.

Treatments

- Early treatment of malaria shortens its duration, prevents complications and lessens the potential of death. Because of its considerable drag on health in low-income countries, malaria disease management is an essential part of global development. Treatment aims to cure patients of the disease rather than diminish the number of parasites carried by an infected person.

- The best available treatment, particularly for *P. falciparum* malaria, is a combination of drugs known as artemisinin-based combination therapies (ACTs). The growing potential for parasite resistance to these medicines, however, is undermining malaria control efforts. There are no effective alternatives to artemisinins for the treatment of malaria either on the market or nearing the end of the drug development process.

Anthrax

Anthrax is a serious disease caused by *Bacillus anthracis*, a bacterium that forms spores. (A bacterium is a very small organism made up of one cell. Many bacteria can cause disease. A spore is a cell that is dormant (asleep) but may come to life with the right conditions.)

There are three types of anthrax:

- Skin (cutaneous)

- Lungs (inhalation)

- Digestive (gastrointestinal)

Transmission

- Anthrax is not known to spread from one person to another.

- Anthrax from animals: Humans can become infected with anthrax by handling products derived from infected animals or by breathing in anthrax spores from infected animal products (like wool, for example). People also can become infected with gastrointestinal anthrax by eating undercooked meat from infected animals.

- Anthrax as a weapon: Anthrax also can be used as a weapon. In the United States in 2001, anthrax was deliberately spread through the postal system by sending letters with powder containing anthrax. This act caused 22 cases of anthrax infection.

How Dangerous Is Anthrax?

- The Centers for Disease Control and Prevention classifies agents with recognized bioterrorism potential into three priority areas (A, B and C). Anthrax is classified as a Category A agent. Category A agents are those that:

  - Pose the greatest possible threat for a detrimental effect on public health

  - May spread across a large area or need public awareness

- Must be met with a great deal of planning in order to protect the public's health

In most cases, early treatment with antibiotics can cure cutaneous anthrax. Even if untreated, 80 percent of people who become infected with cutaneous anthrax do not die. Gastrointestinal anthrax is more serious because between one-fourth to more than half of cases lead to death. Inhalation anthrax is much more severe. In 2001, about half of the cases of inhalation anthrax ended in death.

Symptoms

The symptoms (warning signs) of anthrax are different, depending on the type of the disease:

- *Cutaneous*: The first symptom is a small sore that develops into a blister. The blister then develops into a skin ulcer with a black area in the center. The sore, blister and ulcer do not hurt.

- *Gastrointestinal*: The first symptoms are nausea, loss of appetite, bloody diarrhea and fever, followed by bad stomach pain.

- *Inhalation*: The first symptoms of inhalation anthrax are cold or flu-like symptoms and can include a sore throat, mild fever and muscle aches. Later symptoms include cough, chest discomfort, shortness of breath, tiredness and muscle aches. (Caution: Do not assume that because a person has cold or flu symptoms they have inhalation anthrax.)

How Soon Do Infected People Get Sick?

Symptoms can appear within seven days of coming in contact with the bacterium for all three types of anthrax. For inhalation anthrax, symptoms may appear within a week or take up to 42 days to appear.

Treatment

Antibiotics are used to treat all three types of anthrax. Early identification and treatment are important, as is preventive treatment in the face of suspected exposure.

- Prevention after exposure. If a person is exposed to anthrax but is not yet sick, health-care providers will use antibiotics (such as ciprofloxacin, levofloxacin, doxycycline, or penicillin) combined with the anthrax vaccine to prevent anthrax infection.

- Treatment after infection. Treatment is usually a 60-day course of antibiotics. Success depends on the type of anthrax and how soon treatment begins.

Prevention

There is a vaccine to prevent anthrax, but it is not yet available for the general public. Anyone who may be exposed to anthrax, including certain members of the U.S. armed forces, laboratory workers, and workers who may enter or re-enter contaminated areas, may get the vaccine. In the event of an attack that used anthrax as a weapon, people who were exposed would receive the vaccine.

Botulism

Botulism is a muscle-paralyzing disease caused by a toxin made by a bacterium called *Clostridium botulinum*.

Key Facts

There are three main kinds of botulism:

- Food-borne botulism occurs when a person ingests pre-formed toxins, leading to illness within a few hours to days. Food-borne botulism is a public health emergency because the contaminated food may still be available to other persons besides the patient.

- Infant botulism occurs in a small number of susceptible infants each year who harbor *C. botulinum* in their intestinal tract.

- Wound botulism occurs when wounds are infected with *C. botulinum*, which secretes the toxin.

Symptoms

With food-borne botulism, symptoms begin within six hours to 2 weeks (most commonly between 12 and 36 hours) after eating food that contains the toxin. Symptoms of botulism include double vision, blurred vision, drooping eyelids, slurred speech, difficulty swallowing, dry mouth, and muscle weakness that moves down the body, always affecting the shoulders first, then the upper arms, lower arms, thighs, calves, etc. Paralysis of breathing muscles can cause a person to stop breathing and die unless assistance with breathing (mechanical ventilation) is provided.

Transmission

Botulism is not spread from one person to another. Food-borne botulism can occur in all age groups.

Treatment and Prevention

A supply of antitoxin against botulism is maintained by CDC. The antitoxin is effective in reducing the severity of symptoms if administered early in the course of the disease. Most patients eventually recover after weeks to months of supportive care. In June 2008, a number Dutch tourists on a mini-cruise in Turkey exhibited symptoms of botulism and were repatriated to the Netherlands. Since there was a shortage of antitoxin in the Netherlands, an emergency delivery was shipped from a German manufacturer. The outbreak was traced to the most likely culprit—locally purchased, unprocessed black olives, but no leftovers were available for investigation. It's important to understand that the antitoxin may not be readily available in all countries.

Salmonellosis

Salmonellosis is an infection with bacteria called Salmonella. Most persons infected with Salmonella develop diarrhea, fever, and abdominal cramps 12 to 72 hours after infection. The illness usually lasts four to seven days. Most persons recover without treatment. However, in some persons the diarrhea may be so severe that the patient needs to be hospitalized. In these patients, the Salmonella infection may spread from the intestines to the blood stream, and then to other body sites. The infection can cause death unless the person is treated promptly with antibiotics. The elderly, infants and those with impaired immune systems are more likely to have a severe illness.

Symptoms

Many different kinds of illnesses can cause diarrhea, fever or abdominal cramps. To identify Salmonella as the cause of the illness, laboratory tests must detect Salmonella in the stools of an infected person. These tests are sometimes not performed unless the laboratory is specifically instructed to look for the organism. Once Salmonella has been identified, further testing can determine its specific type, and which antibiotics could be used to treat it.

Treatment

Salmonella infections usually resolve in five to seven days and often do not require treatment unless the patient becomes severely dehydrated or the infection spreads from the intestines. Persons with severe diarrhea may require rehydration, often with intravenous fluids. Antibiotics are not usually necessary unless the infection spreads from the intestines, in which case it can be treated with ampicillin, gentamicin, trimethoprim/sulfamethoxazole, or ciprofloxacin. Unfortunately, some Salmonella bacteria have become resistant to antibiotics, largely as a result of the use of antibiotics to promote growth of feed animals.

Long-term Implications

Persons with diarrhea usually recover completely, although it may be several months before their bowel habits are entirely normal. A small number of persons who are infected with Salmonella will go on to develop pains in their joints, irritation of the eyes, and painful urination. This is called Reiter's syndrome. It can last for months or years and can lead to chronic arthritis, which is difficult to treat. Antibiotic treatment does not make a difference in whether or not the person later develops arthritis.

Transmission

Salmonella live in the intestinal tracts of humans and other animals, including birds, and are usually transmitted to humans via foods contaminated with animal feces. Contaminated foods usually look and smell normal, and are often of animal origin—beef, poultry, milk, or eggs are common examples, but all foods, including vegetables, may become contaminated. Raw foods of animal origin are frequently contaminated, but fortunately, thorough cooking kills Salmonella. Food may also become contaminated by an infected food handler who forgot to wash his or her hands with soap after using the bathroom.

Salmonella may also be found in the feces of some pets, especially those with diarrhea. Individuals can become infected if they do not wash their hands after contact with these feces. Reptiles are particularly likely to harbor Salmonella. People should always wash their hands immediately after handling a reptile, even if the reptile is healthy. Adults should also make sure children wash their hands after handling a reptile.

Prevention

There is no vaccine to prevent salmonellosis. Since foods of animal origin may be contaminated with Salmonella, try not eat raw or undercooked eggs, poultry or meat. Be careful as you may not recognize that raw eggs are in some foods, such as homemade hollandaise sauce, homemade salad dressings, tiramisu, homemade ice cream, homemade mayonnaise, cookie dough and frostings. Poultry and meat, including hamburgers, should be well cooked, not pink in the middle. Try not consume raw or unpasteurized milk or other dairy products. Thoroughly wash produce before consuming.

Avoid cross-contamination of foods. Keep uncooked meats separate from produce, cooked foods and ready-to-eat foods. Thoroughly wash hands, cutting boards, counters, knives, and other utensils after handling uncooked foods. Wash hands before handling any food, and between handling different food items. Individuals who have salmonellosis should not prepare food or pour water for others until they have been shown to no longer carry the Salmonella bacterium. Wash hands after contact with animal feces. Since reptiles are particularly likely to have Salmonella, everyone should immediately wash their hands after handling reptiles. Reptiles (including turtles) are not appropriate pets for small children and should not be in the same house as an infant.

Cholera

Cholera is an acute diarrheal illness caused by infection of the intestine with the bacterium *Vibrio cholerae*. The infection is often mild or without symptoms, but can sometimes be severe. Approximately one in 20 infected persons has severe disease characterized by profuse watery diarrhea, vomiting and leg cramps. In these persons, rapid loss of body fluids leads to dehydration and shock. Without treatment, death can occur within hours. What should travelers do to avoid getting cholera?

The risk for cholera is very low for U.S. travelers visiting areas with epidemic cholera. When simple precautions are observed, contracting the disease is unlikely.

All travelers to areas where cholera has occurred should observe the following recommendations:

Drink only water that you have boiled or treated with chlorine or iodine. Other safe beverages include tea and coffee made with boiled water and carbonated bottled beverages with no ice. Eat only foods that have been thoroughly cooked and are still hot, or fruit that you have peeled yourself. Avoid undercooked or raw fish or shellfish, including ceviche. Make sure all vegetables are cooked. Avoid salads. Avoid foods and beverages from street vendors. Do not bring perishable seafood back to the United States.

A simple rule of thumb is—"Boil it, cook it, peel it, or forget it."

Raids

Criminals hide everywhere, exploiting, thieving and destroying anything they can get their hands on. You may not be singled out for a criminal attack in the United States, but overseas, you better believe that you have a good chance of becoming a target. An increasingly unstable economic situation worldwide means that crime will only increase. Fortunately, Personal Awareness can help you avoid or escape criminal intrigue. In all cases, your actions should be dictated by the reason you are in the country and the perceived risk. Choose your battles wisely to reduce unnecessary attention to yourself. If you are pick-pocketed, ask yourself whether it's really worth chasing the criminal down.

Crimes of interest, as they relate to the traveler, consist of some form of carjacking, kidnapping, or hostage and ransom operations. There are plenty more examples, but these are the crimes with potential for death. Because overseas, a large number of these crimes will be committed when you are approaching your vehicle or while driving, the following section will cover the anatomy of and best responses to carjacking, kidnapping and hostage ransom crimes.

Carjacking

Carjacking has become one of the most prevalent crimes in many parts of the world, overtaking car theft as sophisticated alarm systems with kill switches force car thieves to switch over to carjacking. Most carjacking crimes occur for the sole purpose of taking the car, a crime without a political agenda that does not specifically target Americans. Whoever you are, you can protect yourself by becoming familiar with the methods, ruses and locations commonly used by carjackers.

Avoidance (Alert Mode)

The first step is to avoid an attack. Be in Alert Mode at all times and be aware of your environment. The most likely places for a carjacking are –

- High crime areas

- Less-traveled roads (rural areas)

- Intersections where you must stop

- Isolated areas in parking lots

- Residential driveways and gates

- Traffic jams or congested areas

Learn to avoid these areas and situations, if possible. If not, take steps to prevent an attack by doing the following this protocol:

- In traffic, look around for possible avenues of escape. Keep some distance between your car and the vehicle in front of you—about one-half of your vehicle's length—so you can maneuver easily if necessary. (You should always be able to see the rear tires of the vehicle in front of you.)

- When stopped, use your rear and side view mirrors to stay aware of your surroundings. Keep your doors locked and windows up. This increases your safety and makes it more difficult for an attacker to surprise you.

Accidents are one ruse used by attackers as a prelude to a carjacking. The following are other common attack plans:

The Bump — The attacker bumps the victim's vehicle from behind. The victim gets out to assess the damage and exchange information. The victim's vehicle is then taken.

Good Samaritan — The attacker(s) stage what appears to be an accident. They may simulate an injury. The victim stops to assist, and the vehicle is taken. (As you'll recall, this ruse was attempted on me in Tanzania.)

The Ruse — The vehicle behind the victim flashes its lights or the driver waves to get the victim's attention. The attacker tries to indicate that there is a problem with the victim's car. The victim pulls over, and the vehicle is taken.

The Trap — Carjackers use surveillance to follow the victim home. When the victim pulls into his or her driveway waiting for the gate to open, the attacker pulls up from behind and blocks the victim's car.

- If you are bumped from behind or if someone tries to alert you to a problem with your vehicle, pull over only when you reach a safe public place.

- If you are driving into a gated community, call ahead to have the gate opened. Otherwise wait on the street until the gate is open before turning in and possibly getting trapped.

- Think before stopping to assist in an accident. It may be safer to call and report the location, number of cars involved, and any injuries you observed.

- You can avoid becoming a victim. Ruses and methods, as well as the types of cars most often targeted, differ from country to country. Talk with the regional security officer (RSO) at your embassy about local scams and accident procedures.

- In all cases, keep your cell phone or radio with you, and immediately alert someone about your situation.

During A Carjacking (Crisis Mode)

In most carjacking situations, the attackers are interested only in the vehicle. Try to stay calm. Do not stare at the attacker, as this may seem aggressive and cause them to harm you.

There are two options during an attack—non-resistive/non-confrontational behavior or resistive/confrontational behavior. Your reaction should be based on certain factors:

- Type of attack

- Environment (isolated or public)

- Mental state of attacker (reasonable or nervous)

- Number of attackers

- Weapons

- The presence of children

In non-confrontational situation, you would:

- Give up the vehicle freely.

- Listen carefully to all directions.

- Make no quick or sudden movements that could be construed as a counterattack.

- Always keeps your hands in plain view.

- Tell the attacker of every move in advance.

- Make the attacker aware if children are present. The attacker may be focused only on the driver and not know children are in the car.

In a resistive or confrontational response, you would make a decision to escape or attack the carjacker. Before doing so, consider:

- The mental state of the attacker.

- Possible avenues of escape.

- The number of attackers. There are usually more than one.

- The use of weapons. (Weapons are used in the majority of carjacking situations.)

- In most instances, it is probably safest to give up your vehicle. It's a rental!

After the Attack (Pre-Crisis)

- OODA loop other possible threats.

- If you are in a populated area, immediately go to a safe place.

- After an attack or an attempted attack, you might not be focused on your safety. Get to a safe place before contacting someone to report the incident.

Reporting the Crime

- Describe the event. What time of day did it occur? Where did it happen? How did it happen? Who was involved?

- Describe the attacker(s). Without staring, try to note height, weight, scars or other distinguishing marks, hair and eye color, the presence of facial hair, build (slender, large) and complexion (dark, fair).

- Describe the attacker's vehicle. If possible get the vehicle license number, color, make, model, and year, as well as any marks (scratches, dents, damage) and personal decorations (stickers, colored wheels).

- The golden rule for descriptions is to give only the information you absolutely remember. If you are not sure, don't guess!

Kidnappings

Top locations for kidnappings:

- Mexico

- Phoenix, AZ

- Brazil

- Colombia

- Venezuela

- Philippines

- Nigeria

- Chechnya

- Afghanistan

- Iraq

- Haiti

- India

- Lebanon

- Kenya

Kidnapping is a low-risk, high-return business that is only becoming increasingly common. Kidnappings can take place in public areas where someone may force you quietly by gunpoint into a vehicle. Or they can take place at a hotel or residence, where an assailant uses a weapon to force your cooperation in leaving the premises and entering a vehicle.

Express kidnappings are becoming more popular and have increasingly been seen as a method used by taxi drivers. These kidnappings only last an hour or more, and generally involve forcing the victim to withdraw money from ATM machines.

Virtual kidnappings are done by phone only. A kidnapping never really takes place. The caller claims to have a family member and demands money.

The initial phase of kidnapping is a critical one. It provides one of the best opportunities to escape. If you are in a public area at the time of abduction, make as much commotion as possible to draw attention to the situation. If the abduction takes place at your hotel room, make noise and attempt to arouse the suspicion or concern of hotel employees or of those in neighboring rooms. At the least, the fact that abduction has taken place will be brought to the attention of authorities and the process of notification and search can begin. Otherwise, it could be hours or days before your absence is reported.

Once you have been forced into a vehicle, you may be blindfolded, physically attacked (to cause unconsciousness), drugged, or forced to lie face down on the floor of the vehicle. In some instances, hostages have been forced into trunks or specially built compartments for transporting contraband.

Do not struggle in your confined state. Calm yourself mentally, and concentrate on surviving.

Employ your mind by attempting to visualize the route being taken, taking note of turns, street noise, smells, etc. Try to keep track of the amount of time spent between points.

Once you have arrived at your destination, you may be placed in a temporary holding area before being moved again to a more permanent detention site.

If you are interrogated:

- Retain a sense of pride, but be cooperative.

- Divulge only information that cannot be used against you.

- Do not antagonize your interrogator with obstinate behavior.

- Concentrate on surviving. If you are to be used as a bargaining tool or to obtain ransom, you will be kept alive.

- After reaching what you may presume to be your permanent detention site (you may be moved several more times), quickly settle into the situation.

- Be observant. Notice the details of the room, the sounds of activity in the building and determine the layout of the building by studying what is visible to you. Listen for sounds through walls, windows or out in the streets. Try to distinguish between smells.

- Stay mentally active by memorizing the aforementioned details. Exercise your memory and practice retention.

- Keep track of time. Devise a way to track the day, date and the time, and use it to develop a daily schedule of activities for yourself.

- Know your captors. Memorize their schedule, look for patterns of behavior to be used to your advantage, and identify weaknesses or vulnerabilities.

- Use all of the above information to seek opportunities to escape.

- Remain cooperative. Attempt to establish rapport with your captors or guards. Once a level of communication is achieved, try asking for items that will increase your personal comfort. Make them aware of your needs.

- Stay physically active even if your movement is extremely limited. Use isometric and flexing exercises to keep your muscles toned.

- If you detect the presence of other hostages in the same building, devise ways to communicate.

- DO NOT be uncooperative, antagonistic, or hostile towards your captors. It is a fact that hostages who display this type of behavior are kept captive longer or are singled out for torture or punishment.

- Watch for signs of Stockholm syndrome, which occurs when the captive, because of close proximity and the constant pressures involved, begins to relate to, and empathize with, the captors. In some cases, the hostage become empathetic to the point that he/she actively participates in the activities of the group. You should attempt to establish a friendly rapport with your captors, but maintain your personal dignity and do not compromise your integrity.

- If you are able to escape, attempt to get first to a U.S. Embassy or Consulate to seek protection. If you cannot reach either, go to a host government or friendly government entity.

Hostage Situations

Any traveler could become a hostage. The odds of that happening are extremely low when the number of travelers is compared to the number of people who have actually been taken hostage. However, there is always that slim chance that a traveler could end up being in the wrong place at the wrong time. With this in mind, the traveler should make sure that his/her affairs are in order before going abroad. Items of particular importance to an individual in a hostage situation are an up-to-date will, insurance policy, and power of attorney for the spouse. If these items have been taken care of before departure, the individual will not have to worry about the family's welfare and the hostage can focus all of his/her efforts on the one thing of paramount importance—SURVIVAL!!

Travelers must realize certain dynamics are involved in a hijacking or a kidnapping. To increase survivability, they must understand how these interacting forces affect the end result. Each individual involved in an incident of this type will have an impact on the eventual outcome. One wrong move by either a victim or a perpetrator could easily result in a disaster rather than a peaceful conclusion to the incident.

The first thing a traveler should remember is that he or she is not the only one who is scared and nervous. Everyone involved is in the same emotional state, including the perpetrators. Fear can trigger a disaster. It does not take much to set off a defensive spate of violence for some individuals. It could be a demonstration of violence to reinforce a demand or to incite fear in the minds of the hostages. Whether the violence is motivated by fanaticism or fear, hostage-takers will direct that violence at the person(s) perceived to be a threat or a nuisance.

The following guidelines will help you minimize the possibility of being selected for special attention by the perpetrators and maximize your ability to survive a hostage situation. These recommendations relate to one particular type of hostage situation, an airline hijacking, but have over-arching universal lessons that can be applied to other situations.

Hijacking Survival Guidelines

The physical takeover of the aircraft by hijackers may be characterized by noise, commotion, and possibly shooting and yelling. Or, it may be quiet and methodical, characterized by little more than an announcement by a crewmember. The first few minutes of the hijacking are crucial, and you should try to:

- Stay calm, and encourage others around you to do the same.

- Remember that the hijackers are extremely nervous and are possibly scared.

- Comply with your captor(s)' directions.

- If shooting occurs, keep your head down or drop to the floor.

- Remain alert.

- Be ready to kill the hijackers if possible.

Once the takeover of the aircraft has occurred, you may be separated by citizenship, sex, race, and so on. Your passport may be confiscated and your carry-on luggage ransacked. The aircraft may be diverted to another country. The hijackers may enter into a negotiation phase, which could last for what seems like an indefinite period of time. In addition, the crew may be forced to fly the aircraft to yet another destination.

During this phase, passengers may be used as a bargaining tool in negotiations, lives may be threatened, or a number of passengers may be released in exchange for items like fuel, landing/departure rights or food. This will be the longest phase of the hijacking, and you should keep the following in mind:

- Prepare yourself mentally and emotionally for a long ordeal.

- If you are told to keep your head down or maintain another body position, talk yourself into relaxing into the position. You may need to stay that way for some time.

- Do not attempt to hide your passport or belongings.

- If addressed by the hijackers, respond in a regulated tone of voice.

- Use your time wisely by observing the characteristics and behavior of the hijackers, mentally attach nicknames to each one and notice their dress, facial features and temperaments.

- If you or nearby passengers are in need of assistance because of illness or discomfort, solicit the assistance of a crewmember first. Do not attempt to approach a hijacker unless similar assistance has been rendered by them for other passengers.

- If the hijackers single you out, be responsive but do not volunteer information.

The last phase of the hijacking is resolution. This may occur through a hostage rescue team or a negotiation. In the latter instance, the hijackers may simply surrender to authorities or abandon the aircraft, crew and passengers. In the case of a hostage rescue operation, you may experience a similar situation as when the aircraft was taken over by the hijackers. There will be noise, chaos and possibly shooting as the rescue force regains control of the aircraft. During this time of jeopardy, you should take care and remember the following:

- If you hear shots fired inside or outside the aircraft, immediately assume a protective position. Put your head down or drop to the floor.

- If instructed by a rescue force to move, do so quickly. Put your hands up in the air or behind your head. Make no sudden movements.

- If fire or smoke appears, attempt to get emergency exits open, and use the inflatable slides or exit onto the wing.

- Once you are on the tarmac, follow the instructions of the rescue force or local authorities. If neither is there to guide you, move as quickly as possible away from the aircraft and eventually move toward the terminal or control tower area.

- Expect to be regarded initially as a hijacker or co-conspirator by the rescue force. You will be treated roughly until it is determined by the rescue force that you are not part of the hijacking team.

- Cooperate with local authorities and members of the U.S. Embassy, Consulate or other U.S. agencies in relating information about the hijacking.

- Your contact with family members and travel going forward will be arranged by U.S. authorities as soon as possible.

September 11th and more recent terrorist attacks have changed views considerably. Could you be involved in such acts? Sure, but it's not likely. If it seems like a suicide mission is unfolding, then OODA loop the situation and become the wolf. Again, that doesn't mean you automatically default to fight. Your options are to run and then hide. Fight only if that is the one remaining choice.

Environmental Threats

Environmental threats overseas are no different than such threats in the United States. The infrastructure and warning systems of other countries, however, are dramatically different. Buildings, dams, piers, communication systems, advanced warning systems, media, and other forms of protection and communication are subpar, to say the least, and that's all without taking into account the issue of language barriers. As a result of these deficiencies, natural disasters and other types of environmental threats are even more of a risk. You may not know about incoming storm systems until they are literally on top of you. Once again, you should conduct a country study before departure to identify potential environmental threats and specifics, such as frequency of weather incidents, active seasons or areas, and actions to take.

Hurricane/Typhoon

If a hurricane or typhoon suddenly appears:

- Language permitting, listen to the radio or TV for information.

- Secure your location, close storm shutters, and secure outdoor objects or bring them indoors.

- Turn off utilities if instructed to do so. Otherwise, turn the refrigerator thermostat to its coldest setting and keep its doors closed.

- Turn off propane tanks.

- Avoid using the phone, except for serious emergencies.

- Moor your boat if time permits (when applicable).

- Ensure a supply of water for sanitary purposes, such as cleaning and flushing toilets.

- Fill the bathtub and other large containers with water.

You should evacuate under the following conditions:

- If you are directed by local authorities to do so. Be sure to follow their instructions.

- If your lodging is a temporary structure no matter how well fastened to the ground.

- If you are in a high-rise building. High winds are stronger at higher elevations.

- If you are on the coast, on a floodplain, near a river, or on an inland waterway.

- If you feel you are in danger. You probably are.

If you are unable to evacuate, go to your safe room.

If you do not have one, follow these guidelines:

- Stay indoors and away from windows and glass doors during the hurricane/typhoon.

- Close all interior doors and secure and brace external doors.

- Keep curtains and blinds closed.

- Do not be fooled if there is a lull. If it's the eye of the storm, winds will pick up again.

- Take refuge in a small interior room, closet, or hallway on the lowest level.

- Lie on the floor under a table or another sturdy object.

Tsunami

If you are in a coastal area with a history of earthquakes, a tsunami is always a possibility. Warnings by radio or television or witnessed seismic activity should be taken very seriously, regardless of the population's actions. *If there is noticeable recession in water away from the shoreline, this is Mother Nature's warning to you to move to higher ground. Do it quickly.*

Both the 2004 Indian Ocean earthquake and the 2011 Japanese earthquake were undersea earthquakes of about a 9.0 magnitude. The Indian Ocean earthquake triggered the most devastating tsunami in recorded history. About 230,000 people lost their lives in 11 countries. Indonesia, Sri Lanka, India, and Thailand were hit hardest by the 100-foot waves. A warning system could have saved thousands of lives. Lives could still have been saved had the warnings by Mother Nature been recognized and heeded. Far less casualties were suffered in the Japanese earthquake, despite a similar devastating tsunami. Why? The people had been trained to expect a deadly tsunami after a large earthquake. Many headed for higher ground immediately after the first major tremor. Although the area suffered major property damage, including meltdowns of nuclear reactors, the total number of dead were about 16,000.

Don't be a "Mr. Atala"

Like everyone else in Maullin, Chile, Ramon Atala survived the 1960 Chile earthquake. Mr. Atala was Maullin's most prosperous merchant. Outside of town, he owned a barn and a plantation of Monterey pine. In town, he owned a pier and at least one large building and also had private quarters in a waterfront warehouse. Between the first and second wave of the tsunami that struck Maullin, Mr. Atala entered his warehouse to retrieve something. The second wave of the tsunami hit, and his warehouse was washed away. Mr. Atala's body was never found. It is unclear what he was trying to save. What is clear is that no possession is worth your life. It is important to get to higher ground away from the coast and stay there until it is safe to return.

Winter Storm

Winter storms are common to some people, and completely foreign to others. You are often most vulnerable to unexpected weather when driving, especially in a foreign country. The following are some key survival tips.

If stranded in a snowstorm:

- Pull off the highway. Turn on hazard lights and hang a distress flag from the radio antenna or window.

- Remain in your vehicle where rescuers are most likely to find you.

- Do not set out on foot unless you can see a building close by where you know you can take shelter. Be careful. Distances are distorted by blowing snow. A building may seem close. It may be too far away in deep snow.

- Run the engine and heater about 10 minutes of each hour to keep warm. When the engine is running, open a downwind window slightly for ventilation and periodically clear snow from the exhaust pipe. This will protect you from possible carbon monoxide poisoning.

- Exercise to maintain body heat, but avoid overexertion. In extreme cold, use road maps, seat covers, and floor mats for insulation. Huddle with passengers and use your coat for a blanket.

- Take turns sleeping. One person should be awake at all times to look for rescue crews.

- Drink fluids to avoid dehydration.

- Be careful not to waste battery power. Balance electrical energy needs—the use of lights, heat, and radio—with supply.

- Turn on the inside light at night so work crews or rescuers can see you.

- If stranded in a remote area, stomp large block letters in an open area spelling out HELP or SOS and line with rocks or tree limbs to attract the attention of rescue personnel who may be surveying the area by airplane.

- Leave the car and proceed on foot, if necessary, once the blizzard passes.

Structural Fire

Fire safety, at home and abroad, is a matter of thinking ahead, knowing what to do, and keeping your fear under control. Panic and smoke are the most dangerous threats in the case of a fire. To minimize the risk of being trapped during a fire, the traveler should remember the precautions listed below (when feasible):

- Stay only at hotels with smoke detectors and/or sprinklers installed in all rooms. The hotel should provide information about fire and safety procedures.

- Request a room between the second and seventh floor. Most fire departments do not have the capability to rescue people above the seventh floor level with ladder rescue equipment.

- Ask the hotel desk clerk how guests are notified if there is an emergency.

Your Hotel Room

- Note the location of the fire exits (stairs) on your floor. Count the number of doors between your room and the exit. If there is a fire, you may have to crawl there in the dark.

- Check exit doors to be sure that they are unlocked and that stairwells are clear of obstructions.

- Note the location of fire alarms, extinguishers and hoses. Read any fire safety information available in your room.

- Check outside your room window to ascertain if there is a possible escape route that would be feasible in an extreme emergency.

In Case of a Fire

- KEEP CALM. DO NOT PANIC.

- Call the front desk and notify them of the location of the fire, if you know.

- Check your door by placing your palm on the door and then on the doorknob. If either feels hot, DO NOT OPEN THE DOOR.

- If it is safe to exit from your room, head for the stairs. TAKE YOUR ROOM KEY WITH YOU. YOU MAY HAVE TO RETURN TO YOUR ROOM.

- If the corridor is full of smoke, crawl to the exit and again check the exit door before opening it to see if it is hot. The fire could be in the stairwell.

- DO NOT USE THE ELEVATOR!

If you cannot leave your room or the stairwells are unsafe and you must return to your room:

- Notify the front desk that you are in your room waiting to be rescued.

- Open a window for fresh air. Do not break the window as you may need to close it again if smoke starts to enter from the outside.

- Fill the tub and sink with water. Soak towels and blankets as necessary to block vents and openings around doors to keep the smoke and fumes out.

- Attempt to keep the walls, doors and cracks covered with towels that are cool and wet.

- A wet towel swung around the room will help clear the air of smoke.

- Cover your mouth and nose with a wet cloth.

- Stay low, but alert to any signs of rescue from the street or the halls. Let the firefighters know where you are by waving a towel or sheet out the window.

An excellent resource for fire-safety information is the National Fire Protection Association (NFPA), an international nonprofit organization that provides guidance on fire, electrical and building codes, and fire safety education and research (www.nfpa.org).

Agencies

Intelligence and law enforcement agencies are always considered a threat, regardless of whether they are hostile or not. *Don't think in terms of just the agencies within the country you are visiting.* Other countries' agencies could be working there as well. If you're a businessperson and think they want nothing to do with you, think again. In today's globalized economy and advanced technology, country borders are nonexistent in the business world. National intelligence and law enforcement agencies are playing bigger and bigger roles in corporate espionage, which is a precursor to economic espionage. And it doesn't take long before economic espionage manifests into sabotage.

After the fall of the Soviet Union, jobless spies hawked their services to the corporate world to vet contacts, pitch sources, and obtain competitors' intellectual property, trade secrets and technology. Soon, governments saw the value of these endeavors. After all, money does make the world go around. If a government can steal IBM's next nano-processor before it hits the market, reverse engineer it, and put it on the market the same day as IBM, that's real power. The French government has allegedly conducted industrial espionage against American aerodynamics and satellite companies for years. Then, over the last 15 years, the French have sold that information to the following countries: Argentina, Brazil, India, Iran, Iraq, Israel, Japan, Lebanon, Libya, North Korea, Pakistan, People's Republic of China, the former USSR (Russia), South Africa, South Korea, and Taiwan. Some are known enemies, and some are "allies." Heck, remember when our economy was doing really well? That's when the CIA was heavily involved in economic warfare...that's also why Osama bin Laden was completely overlooked.

The Cold War is not over. It has merely moved into a new arena: the global marketplace. The FBI estimates that every year billions of U.S. dollars are lost to foreign competitors who deliberately target economic intelligence in flourishing U.S. industries and technologies and who cull intelligence out of shelved technologies by exploiting open source and classified information known as trade secrets. Foreign competitors who criminally seek economic intelligence generally operate in three ways to create their spy networks:

1. They aggressively target and recruit susceptible people (often from the same national background) working for U.S. companies and research institutions.

2. They recruit people to locate economic intelligence through operations like bribery, discreet theft, dumpster diving (in search of discarded trade secrets) and wiretapping.

3. They establish seemingly innocent business relationships between foreign companies and U.S. industries to gather economic intelligence, including classified information.

In an effort to safeguard our nation's economic secrets, the Economic Espionage Act (EEA) was signed into law on October 11, 1996. You can also take action to protect your business interests when traveling.

How to Protect Your Business from Espionage: Six Steps

1. Recognize there is a real threat.

2. Identify and evaluate trade secrets.

3. Implement a definable plan for safeguarding trade secrets.

4. Secure physical trade secrets and limit access to trade secrets.

5. Confine intellectual knowledge.

6. Provide ongoing security training to employees.

Law enforcement research is paramount, because some of the most prolific criminals in other countries are the police. Police corruption is a specific form of police misconduct in which the crimes are usually financially orientated and harmless. The most common form of corruption is the solicitation of or acceptance of bribes. If you travel to our closest threat country, Mexico, chances are high that you will be stopped by the police and "fined" exactly what happens to be in your wallet. In some countries, the police play large roles in the trafficking of drugs, humans and terrorists. So beware and research your destination.

Definitions

Economic espionage is (1) whoever knowingly performs targeting or acquisition of trade secrets to (2) knowingly benefit any foreign government, foreign instrumentality, or foreign agent. (Title18 U.S.C., Section 1831).

Trade secrets cover all forms and types of financial, business, scientific, technical, economic or engineering information, including patterns, plans, compilations, program devices, formulas, designs, prototypes, methods, techniques, processes, procedures, programs, or codes—whether tangible or intangible, and whether they are stored, compiled, or memorialized physically, electronically, graphically, photographically or in writing—which the owner has taken reasonable measures to protect, and which have an independent economic value. Trade secrets are commonly called classified proprietary information, economic policy information, trade information, proprietary technology or critical technology.

Theft of trade secrets occurs when someone (1) knowingly performs targeting or acquisition of trade secrets or intends to convert a trade secret to (2) knowingly benefit anyone other than the owner. This is commonly referred to as ***industrial espionage***. (Title 18 U.S.C., SECTION 1832).

A ***foreign agent*** is any officer, employee, proxy, servant, delegate or representative of a foreign government.

A ***foreign instrumentality*** is defined as: (1) any agency, bureau, ministry, component, institution or association; (2) any legal commercial or business organization, corporation, firm, or entity; that is, (3) substantially owned, controlled, sponsored, commanded, managed or dominated by a foreign government.

Terrorism

"The key factors that spawned international terrorism show no signs of abating over the next 15 years.... Lagging economies, ethnic affiliations, intense religious convictions, and youth bulges will align to create a 'perfect storm,' creating conditions likely to spawn internal conflict. The governing capacity of states, however, will determine whether and to what extent conflicts actually occur. Those states unable both to satisfy the expectations of their peoples and to resolve or quell conflicting demands among them are likely to encounter the most severe and most frequent outbreaks of violence." [National Intelligence Council, December 2004.]

With a global economic downfall and terrorism on the climb, the National Intelligence Council may have been correct in 2004. America's reputation is at an all-time low. Terrorism feeds on global discontent with the United States and allows potential terrorists to commit to destroying themselves in the name of a cause or religion. It's important to study which terrorist organizations exist along your route overseas and at your destination. In this chapter, I will highlight some key facts on terrorists, terrorist groups and specific tactics.

Myth vs. Reality

- *Myth:* Poverty is the primary breeding ground for terrorism.

- *Reality:* Many terrorists come from middle-class families and typically have college degrees. Most of their degrees are in the technical sciences and engineering. Terrorists really have no common ground other than motivation.

- *Myth:* U.S. foreign policy drives radicalization.

- *Reality:* Radicalization usually stems from local frustrations caused by international events. Radicalization causes are diverse and vary by location and group.

- *Myth:* All terrorists are Muslim.

- *Reality:* Terrorist motivations are vast. There are hundreds of terrorist organizations that use the same tactics for a variety of reasons. The motivations, just to list a few, include religion, nationalism, anarchism, Leftism, communism, Leninism, Maoism, Marxism, ethnic terrorism (which includes neo-Nazis and white-supremacists), anti-communism, Cuban exile groups, and issue-specific groups (like eco-terrorists and anti-abortion extremists).

Sunni vs. Shiites

There are two main branches within the Islamic faith. The Sunni branch of Islam believes that the first four caliphs, Mohammed's successors, rightfully took his place as leaders of Islam. They recognize the heirs who ruled continuously in the Arab world until the breakup of the Ottoman Empire following World War I. They represent the vast majority of Muslims in the world.

The Shiites believe that only the heir of the fourth caliph, Ali, is the legitimate successor of Mohammed, and that there were no other legitimate religious figures after the fourth caliph, in 931, until Ayatollah Ruhollah Khomeini in 1978. Although in the minority of Muslims worldwide, the Shiites are in the majority in Iran and Iraq and also have sizable representation in Yemen, Pakistan, Syria, Lebanon, East Africa and northern India.

Most Muslims do not identify themselves as one or the other group, but when traveling, it's important to understand that the two groups do have differences in prayer, fasting, pilgrimage and other aspects of daily life. And, in certain locations, like Iraq, the groups have engaged in bitter conflict.

Ramadan-Related Information

As many people know, Islam requires that Ramadan, the ninth month of the Muslim calendar, be devoted to fasting and prayer. During this month, Muslims fast from dawn to sunset each day and eat only small meals in the evening. What many people don't know is that though Muslims are banned from fighting other Muslims during Ramadan, they may engage in combat with non-Muslims. This is why Islamic extremists have extolled Ramadan as a month of jihad, or holy war, against nonbelievers. Many Islamic extremists believe that suicide operations ("martyrdom"), especially if done during Ramadan, guarantee the operative a place in paradise.

When traveling in a location with a large Muslim population, you should be aware of when this holiday falls and be respectful of the local customs. You should also be very cautious to avoid attracting unwarranted Third Party Awareness.

Night of Power (Laylat al-Qadr) Islamic extremists might consider Laylat al-Qadr ("Night of Power") especially auspicious for a terrorist attack. Islamic tradition holds that on this night rewards for deeds pleasing to Allah are magnified a thousand fold. Extremists, in particular, believe that the gates of heaven are opened then for those who wage "jihad" in defense of Islam to enter paradise. While there is much debate, Islamic scholars generally agree that the most likely date for Laylat al-Qadr to occur each year is the evening of the 27th day of Ramadan—the anniversary of Allah's first revelation to the Prophet Muhammad of the Quran. However, many scholars believe that other likely dates for Laylat al-Qadr are the evenings of the 21st, 23rd, 25th, or 29th day of Ramadan. Some scholars teach that any of the last 10 evenings of Ramadan are potential dates for Laylat al-Qadr. Again, you may want to look up those potential dates on the Internet to see if they fall within the timeline of your planned trip.

The Battle of Badr A second date during the month when Islamic extremists might consider it auspicious to attack is the anniversary of the Battle of Badr, the 17th day of Ramadan. Muhammad and his army fought this battle against non-Islamic combatants in the face of overwhelming odds. It is considered to have laid the foundation for the Islamic state.

The Lunar Calendar and Holiday Observance The Islamic calendar is based on the movement and observation of the moon. The Islamic year contains 12 months, none of which can exceed 30 days. Each month starts when the lunar crescent is first seen after a new moon. Because 12 lunar months multiplied by 29.53 days equals 354.36 days, the Islamic calendar will always be approximately 11 days shorter than the Western, or Gregorian, calendar. As explained in the footnotes of this calendar, holidays begin the sundown of the previous day. Because of lunar observation and differences in time zones, the observance of Islamic holidays may vary from region to region.

Islamic Fundamentalist Terror Organizations

ISIL/ISIS – Location: Global. The group originated as Jama'at al-Tawhid wal-Jihad in 1999, which pledged allegiance to al-Qaeda in 2004. This organization participated in the Iraqi insurgency, which followed the March

2003 invasion of Iraq by Western forces. In January 2006, it joined other Sunni insurgent groups to form the Mujahideen Shura Council, which proclaimed the formation of the Islamic State of Iraq (ISI) in October 2006. After the Syrian Civil War began in March 2011, the ISI, under the leadership of al-Baghdadi, sent delegates into Syria in August 2011. These fighters named themselves Jabhat an-Nuṣrah li-Ahli ash-Shām—al-Nusra Front—and established a large presence in Sunni-majority areas of Syria, within the governorates of Ar-Raqqah, Idlib, Deir ez-Zor, and Aleppo. In April 2013, al-Baghdadi announced the merger of the ISI with al-Nusra Front and that the name of the reunited group was now the Islamic State of Iraq and the Levant (ISIL). However, Abu Mohammad al-Julani and Ayman al-Zawahiri, the leaders of al-Nusra and al-Qaeda respectively, rejected the merger. After an eight-month power struggle, al-Qaeda cut all ties with ISIL citing its failure to consult and "notorious intransigence." In Syria, the group has conducted ground attacks on both government forces and rebel factions in the Syrian Civil War. The group gained prominence after it drove Iraqi government forces out of key cities in western Iraq in an offensive initiated in early 2014. Iraq's territorial loss almost caused a collapse of the Iraqi government and prompted a renewal of US military action in Iraq.

> **ISIL tactics:** is adept at social media, posting Internet videos of beheadings of soldiers, civilians, journalists and aid workers, and is known for its destruction of cultural heritage sites. In addition to hostage taking and brutal murders, ISIL's "call to action" has prompted many "Loan Wolf" actors to create as much mayhem and murder as possible in countries around the world. Recently, the group has evolved its tactics to charge regional leaders with planning and executing major terrorism attacks, such as the November 2015 Paris massacre.

Muslim leaders have condemned ISIL's ideology and actions, arguing that the group has strayed from the path of true Islam and that its actions do not reflect the religion's true teachings or virtues. The group's adoption of the name "Islamic State" and idea of a caliphate have been widely criticized, with the United Nations, NATO, various governments, and mainstream Muslim groups rejecting both. It should be noted that although ISIL and Al-Qaeda are basically at war with each other, however always remember the ancient proverb *"The enemy of my enemy is my friend."*

Al-Qaeda – Location: Global. Established in 1988 by Osama Bin Laden with Arabs who fought in Afghanistan against the Russians, Al-Qaeda's goal is uniting Muslims to fight the West, especially the United States. In the mind of this terrorist organization, attacking the West will lead to the destruction of Israel. Al-Qaeda also wants to spread Islam throughout the world and establish a pan-Islamic caliph.

> **Al Qaeda tactics** – Capture of four U.S. commercial jets and crashing them into U.S. symbols of democracy – 3,000 dead. Suicide bombing of the USS Cole with an explosive-laden boat – 17 sailors dead. U.S. Embassy bombings in Nairobi and Tanzania – 224 dead, and many other attacks.

Abu Sayyaf Group (ASG) – Location: Philippines. ASG is the most violent of the Islamic separatists operating out of the southern Philippines. Originally attached to the Moro National Liberation Front, but split off in 1990s, ASG uses terror for profit and to promote its jihadist agenda.

> **ASG tactics** – The organization currently engages in kidnappings for ransom, bombings, assassinations and extortion. Its members have ties to the Jemaah Islamiya (JI) based out of Indonesia. They successfully bombed a ferry in Manila – 116 dead. Simultaneous bombings in 3 major cities killed eight and injured 150. More recently, they engaged the Philippine Marines, killing 14, 10 of whom were beheaded. They also killed members of the Philippine Congress with a motorcycle bomb.

But there are other groups, apart from radical Muslims, that want Americans dead as well.

Revolutionary Armed Forces of Columbia (FARC) – Location: Columbia. Established in 1964 as the military wing of the Columbian Communist Party, the Revolution Armed Forces of Columbia is Latin America's oldest, largest and best-equipped insurgency of Marxist origin. It normally fights in support of Marxist goals. The FARC primarily operates inside Columbia with some kidnapping, weapons sourcing and logistics in neighboring countries.

> **FARC tactics** – FARC uses bombings, murder, mortar attacks, kidnapping, extortion, hijacking, and guerrilla and conventional military action against Columbian political, military and economic targets. It also has heavy ties to narcotic trafficking, cultivation and distribution. FARC considers U.S. citizens legitimate targets because of U.S. support for the Columbian government.

Revolutionary People's Liberation Party/Front (DHKP/C) – Location: Turkey. Established in 1978 as the Devrimci Sol, or Dev Sol, a splinter faction of Dev Genc. Ideological terrorist group with strong Marxist-Leninist values that passionately dislikes the United States, NATO and the Turkish government. Primary goal is to establish a Socialist state and the elimination of F-type (high-security) prisons.

> *DHKP/C tactics* – DHKP are more surgical in attacks primarily against former Turkish government and military officials. Improvised explosives have been the group's primary weapon, although in 2001, these terrorists added suicide bombings to their inventory.

As you know, there are plenty more terrorist organizations that span the globe. Hezbollah and Hamas are among the more visible. Awareness is more than just keeping track of your surroundings. Take ownership of your travels by researching possible threats ahead of time.

Terrorist-Specific Tactics

Bioterrorism - A bioterrorism attack is the deliberate release of viruses, bacteria or other germs (agents) to cause illness or death in people, animals or plants. These agents are typically found in nature, but sometimes altered to increase their ability to cause disease, make them resistant to current medicines, or further their spread into the environment. Biological agents can be spread through air, water or food.

Terrorists may use biological agents because they can be extremely difficult to detect and do not cause illness for several hours to several days. Some bioterrorism agents, like the smallpox virus, can be spread from person to person. Some, like anthrax, cannot.

Suicide Bombers - In a suicide attack upon a target, the attacker intends to kill others and cause great damage, knowing that he or she will either certainly, or most likely, die in the process. These attacks can use explosive laden vests, vehicles, aircraft or vessels. Although recent history has focused on Muslims and their individual quests to martyrdom, these tactics have been going on since the beginning of time. Just 60 years ago, the Japanese were using submarines and aircraft (kaiten and kamikaze) to cause the same effects. One group does it for God and possible rewards in the afterlife, and the other for honor and country.

Alerting Signs of a Suicide Bomber:

- Tunnel vision

- Intense stare

- Poor projection

- Clothing may not match season

- A visible vest hidden under clothing

- Exposed wires or trigger in hand

- Mumbling or rambling in prayer

If you see signs of a possible suicide bomber, make it known. Take cover. And pray for a dud.

Beheadings – Muslim terror groups use beheadings not only for the fear factor, but also to fulfill their interpretation of the Quran. For centuries, leading Islamic scholars have interpreted this verse literally. The famous Iranian historian and Quran commentator Muhammad, b. Jarir at-Tabari (d. 923 C.E.), wrote that "striking at the necks" is simply God's sanction of ferocious opposition to non-Muslims. Mahmud, b. Umar az-Zamakhshari (d. 1143 C.E.), in a major commentary studied for centuries by Sunni religious scholars, suggested that any prescription to "strike at the necks" commands to avoid striking elsewhere so as to confirm death and not simply wound. The practice of beheading non-Muslim captives extends back to the Prophet himself. Ibn Ishaq (d. 768 C.E.), the earliest biographer of Muhammad, is recorded as saying that the Prophet ordered the execution by decapitation of 700 men of the Jewish Banu Qurayza tribe in Medina for allegedly plotting against him. Islamic leaders from Muhammad's time have followed his model. Examples of decapitation, of both the living and the dead, in Islamic history are myriad.

The Dirty Bomb - A dirty bomb is a mix of explosives, such as dynamite, with radioactive powder or pellets. When the dynamite or other explosives are set off, the blast carries radioactive material into the surrounding area. A dirty bomb is *not* the same as an atomic bomb. An atomic bomb, like the bombs dropped on Hiroshima and Nagasaki, Japan, involves the splitting of atoms and a huge release of energy, which produces an atomic mushroom cloud.

A dirty bomb works completely differently and *cannot create an atomic blast.* Instead, a dirty bomb uses dynamite or other explosives to scatter radioactive dust, smoke, or other material and cause radioactive contamination.

What Are the Main Dangers of a Dirty Bomb?

The main danger from a dirty bomb is from the explosion, which can cause serious injuries and property damage. The radioactive materials used in a dirty bomb would probably not create enough radiation exposure to cause immediate serious illness, except for individuals who are very close to the blast site. As the radioactive dust and smoke spreads farther away, it could be dangerous if inhaled. Because you cannot see, smell, feel, or taste radiation, you should take immediate steps to protect yourself and your loved ones.

What Immediate Actions Should you take to Protect Yourself?

These simple steps, recommended by doctors and radiation experts, will help protect you. What actions you take depend on where you are located when the incident occurs—outside, inside, or in a vehicle.

If You Are Outside and Close to the Incident:

- Cover your nose and mouth with a cloth to reduce the risk of breathing in radioactive dust or smoke.

- Don't touch objects thrown off by an explosion. They might be radioactive.

- Quickly go into a building where the walls and windows have not been broken. This area will shield you from radiation that might be outside.

- Once you are inside, take off your outer layer of clothing and seal it in a plastic bag if available. Put the cloth you used to cover your mouth in the bag, too. Removing outer clothes may get rid of up to 90% of radioactive dust.

- Put the plastic bag where others will not touch it and keep it until authorities tell you what to do with it.

- Shower or wash with soap and water. Be sure to wash your hair. Washing will remove any remaining dust.

- Tune to the local radio or television news for more instructions.

If You Are Inside and Close to the Incident:

- If the walls and windows of the building are not broken, stay in the building and do not leave.

- To keep radioactive dust or powder from getting inside, shut all windows, outside doors, and fireplace dampers. Turn off fans and heating and air-conditioning systems that bring in air from the outside. It is not necessary to put duct tape or plastic around doors or windows.

- If the walls and windows of the building are broken, go to an interior room and do not leave. If the building has been heavily damaged, quickly go into a building where the walls and windows have not been broken. If you must go outside, be sure to cover your nose and mouth with a cloth. Once you are inside, take off your outer layer of clothing and seal it in a plastic bag if available. Store the bag where others will not touch it.

- Shower or wash with soap and water, removing any remaining dust. Be sure to wash your hair.

- Tune to local radio or television news for more instructions.

If You Are in a Car When the Incident Happens:

- Close the windows and turn off the air conditioner, heater and vents.

- Cover your nose and mouth with a cloth to avoid breathing radioactive dust or smoke.

- If you are close to your home, office or a public building, go there immediately and go inside quickly.

- If you cannot get to your home or another building safely, pull over to the side of the road and stop in the safest place possible. If it is a hot or sunny day, try to stop under a bridge or in a shady spot.

- Turn off the engine and listen to the radio for instructions.

- Stay in the car until you are told it is safe to get back on the road.

Will Food and Water Supplies Be Safe?

- Food and water supplies most likely will remain safe. Any unpackaged food or water out in the open and close to the incident may have radioactive dust on it. Therefore, do not consume water or food that was out in the open.

- The food inside of cans and other sealed containers will be safe to eat. Wash the outside of the container before opening it.

How Do I Know if I've Been Exposed to Radiation or Contaminated by Radioactive Materials?

- People cannot see, smell, feel, or taste radiation. So you may not know whether you have been exposed. Police or firefighters will quickly check for radiation by using special equipment to determine how much radiation is present and whether it poses any danger in your area.

Low levels of radiation exposure (like those expected from a dirty bomb situation) do not cause any symptoms. Higher levels of radiation exposure may produce symptoms, such as nausea, vomiting, diarrhea, and swelling and redness of the skin. If you develop any of these symptoms, you should contact your doctor, hospital or other sites recommended by authorities.

"There are only two emotions in a plane: boredom and terror."
—Orson Welles

Chapter 6 Review
Practice Assignment – THREATs

When Preparation Pays Off

In this chapter, we've explored the various types of environmental threats. Some are natural, and some are manmade. All can be lethal, if you aren't prepared to avoid or minimize the risks associated with them. It's a matter of proper preparation before you even pick up your suitcase. When traveling, you then need to practice good Situational Awareness, Personal Awareness and Third Party Awareness.

Now let's see how to apply those skills to a hypothetical situation.

Practical Example

- Semi-permissive environment (area with some government control).

- Vacationing in a popular resort area in a remote area of Greece.

You recently arrived at a nice resort area and checked into your bungalow. Just as you step out into the sun, you feel a tremor. The shaking doesn't stop for what seems like an eternity. The wood in your bungalow starts to creak, and rocks from the cliffs nearby start to tumble. People start running out into the streets, screaming. Then, suddenly, everything is quiet. You've just gone through a major earthquake. There's no electricity, no services, no transportation. A number of people in the local community have been hurt or killed. You're lucky to have come through without injury. But what do you do now?

Study Guide Questions

What preparations could you have made before beginning your trip that would have helped you cope with a disaster scenario?

How will you find food, water and shelter until you can identify a way to leave the scene of the disaster?

Study Guide Answers

What preparations could you have made before beginning your trip that would have helped you cope with a disaster scenario?

Before leaving home, you had the foresight to educate yourself about the overall environment and the types of threats that were present. In this case, while thoroughly researching your lovely resort area, you would have come across the information that Greece is one of the world's most seismically active countries. Although most Greek earthquakes are mild, there is always the potential for more severe seismic activity.

You would have taken steps to register with the U.S. Embassy in Greece, so the government would know you were at the resort. You might also have signed up for the U.S. Geological Survey's earthquake notification service and had text notifications sent to your cell phone (which you checked to make sure would work in Greece). As a result, you would have learned of a few earlier, smaller tremors. So you weren't totally unprepared.

How would you find food, water and shelter until you can identify a way to leave the scene of the disaster?

You would also be carrying a list of emergency contact numbers, including local emergency services, hospitals and embassies or consulates. Since you don't speak Greek, you would have a list of emergency words and phrases that would come in very handy when asking for assistance, food and water.

You'd have taken time to scope out shelter in your bungalow, the exterior area and an evacuation route for after the earthquake. You would have determined how to get to higher ground since you are staying near the ocean—just in case the earthquake triggered a tsunami.

It will be a challenging couple of days, but thanks to advance preparation and your ability to make good decisions in the moment, you will come through the incident unscathed.

NOTES:

References Chapter 6

Business Travel Abroad, Department of State, Overseas Security Council, Diplomatic Publications, Released 1994.

Burton, Fred. Stewart, Scott. Threats, Situational Awareness and Perspective, Terrorism Intelligence Report, August 2007.

Carjacking: Don't be a Victim, Overseas Security Advisory Council, Department of State, OSAC Publication 2005.

Centers for Disease Control and Prevention, Division of Global Migration and Quarantine, National Center for Preparedness, Detection, and Control of Infectious Diseases, Atlanta GA, 2009.

C.M. Swaan, C. M. Van Ouwerkerk, I.M. Roest, H.J. Eurosurveillance, Volume 15, Issue 14, 08 April 2010, Cluster of Botulism Among Dutch Tourists in Turkey, June 2008.

Counterterrorism, The National Counterterrorism Center, Counterterrorism Calendar, September 2008.

OnGuardOnline www.onguardonline.gov.

The National Fire Protection Association www.nfpa.org.

The Red Cross www.redcross.org.

Chapter 7

Travel Preparation and Planning

*"A journey is like marriage.
The certain way to be wrong is to think you control it."*
—John Steinbeck

By now, you're well aware of the various different ways that traveling professionals can become targets for criminal and terrorist attacks and environmental threats. But as you understand by now, there are important steps you can take to protect yourself *before* you travel. Based primarily on U.S. State Department information, this chapter discusses security-conscious travel planning and preparation.

Country Study and Research

It pays to use the Total Awareness system to plan out your trip from beginning to end. Personal, Cultural, Third Party, and THREAT assessments must be done to increase your overall Situational Awareness. Know the environments (permissive, semi-permissive, or non-permissive) and threats that you could potentially face. Understand the culture and adapt your Personal Awareness accordingly. Write out THREAT on a piece of paper and look each type of threat up. Like G.I. Joe, "knowing is half the battle."

Travel Itinerary

DO NOT publicize your travel plans. In this age of social media, this precaution has become all the more important. Too many people want to post their travel plans on Facebook or other social media outlets, making themselves potential victims. Limit that knowledge to those who need to know. Leave a full itinerary of your travel schedule, hotel phone numbers and business appointments with your office and with a family member or friend.

Passport

Is your passport valid? Are visas current for the country of destination? If not, you and everything in your possession may be looked at in-depth by host government authorities. If you are carrying sensitive or proprietary documents, they will be examined in detail to see if they reveal any interesting material. If they do, you can bet copies will be made. There will not be much you can do about it.

Make photocopies of your passport, visa and other important travel documents. Keep copies in both your carry-on and checked luggage. This makes it easier to replace your identification documents in the event that should anything happen. (It is also a good idea to leave a photocopy of these documents with someone at home.)

If your passport has the radio-frequency identification (RFID) symbol on the front, make sure you have some foil to wrap it up with, or enclose it in in a case that blocks RFID readers and protects against identity theft. *Escape the Wolf* offers the Zero Trace™ line of patented RFID products, with a foolproof seal designed by a Navy SEAL.

Visas

Is a visa required for any countries you are visiting? Do you have the appropriate visa(s)? Is the information on your visa application true and correct? In some countries, falsifying information on a visa application can result in an unexpected vacation in the local bastilles.

Some countries are sensitive about the type of visa you obtain. If you are traveling on business, a business visa should be obtained. Otherwise, a tourist visa is acceptable.

Medical

Take an adequate supply of any prescription medication with you, as well as an extra set of eyeglasses or contact lenses. Ideally, prescriptions should be in their original containers. Also, take a copy of eyeglasses and medical prescription(s) should you need to have anything replaced. Maintain your inoculation record and update it before each trip, as each country has different requirements.

Make a list of essential medical information—your blood type, allergies, medical conditions and special requirements—and carry it with you. It is a good idea to have a medical alert bracelet if you have a special medical condition.

Does the country you are visiting require any specific inoculations? As an example, most western African countries require proof of a yellow fever inoculation. This information is available from embassies or consulates. Be sure to carry your international vaccination record, just in case.

If you do not have comprehensive medical coverage, consider enrolling in an international health program. You may even choose to do this even if you do have coverage. Some policies don't cover emergency medical evacuations, which can run into tens of thousands of dollars. Hospitals in foreign countries usually do not take credit cards, and most will not honor U.S.-based medical insurance plans.

Miscellaneous

- Keep your personal affairs up to date. If possible, leave a power of attorney with a family member or friend in case anything should happen to you.

- Research the country you will be traveling to before you go. Talk with friends, family or business associates who have visited the country. They can usually give you some good tips for your trip. To learn about any other travel warnings or other conditions, check with the U.S. State Department, Bureau of Consular Affairs.

- Travelers should discuss with their travel agents which airlines, hotels and car rental companies are recommended.

- Consider obtaining a modest amount of foreign currency before you leave your home country. Criminals often watch for and target international travelers purchasing large amounts of foreign currency at airport banks and currency exchange windows.

- Carry only the documents you will need in your wallet/pocketbook. Take only the credit cards you plan to use on your trip.

- If you plan to rent a car, check to see if you must obtain an international driver's permit for the country you plan to visit.

- Obtain information from U.S. Customs regarding any special requirements for the country you are visiting.

Local Import Restrictions

Request any lists or pamphlets describing customs restrictions or banned materials from the embassy of the country you plan to visit. This is designed to minimize the possibility of an encounter with the local authorities. Leave all expensive and heirloom jewelry at home.

Luggage

DO NOT pack sensitive or proprietary information in your checked luggage. Double-envelope sensitive material and hand carry it. Be sure that your luggage is tagged with covered tags to protect your address from open observation. Put your name and address inside each piece of luggage. Be sure all luggage is locked or secured in some fashion.

- DO NOT pack extra glasses or necessary daily medication in your luggage. Carry these items in your briefcase, purse or pocket. If your luggage is lost or you are the victim of a hijacking, you may need these items.

- On your luggage, use your business address and telephone number. If possible, use a nametag with a cover. Do not use a laminated business card on your luggage, and avoid displaying your company's name or any logos on your luggage.

- Check with the airline and/or your personal insurance company regarding any lost luggage coverage.

- Make sure you use sturdy luggage. Do not over-pack, as the luggage could open if dropped. Bind the luggage with strapping to keep it intact.

- Never place valuables (jewelry, money and travelers checks) in your checked luggage. Never leave your bags unattended.

Luggage Locks

The locks on your luggage are really no more than a deterrent. For professional thief or manipulator, no luggage lock is secure. But if time is of the essence to the perpetrator, as it usually is when a crime is involved, here are a couple of suggestions that might deter surreptitious entry and/or theft:

- For added security on all luggage, run a strip of nylon filament tape around the suitcase to preclude its opening accidentally if dropped or mistreated by baggage handlers.

- For luggage and briefcases with two combination locks, reset the combination locks from the factory combination (000) to different combinations on each of the right and left locks.

- For luggage with single locks, set the lock on each piece of luggage with a different combination.

- A TSA-accepted luggage lock allows baggage screeners and security agents to open your suitcase for inspection using a universal master key. A number of manufacturers offer TSA-accepted locks under various brand names. The TSA requires packaging to clearly state that the lock is accepted and recognized by the agency and may be opened by a TSA master key. When shopping for a TSA-accepted lock, look for the Travel Sentry or Safe Skies logo on the packaging. The Travel Sentry logo is a red diamond. The Safe Skies mark is a red torch.

Airline Security and Seat Selection

- Try to book a non-stop flight, as these have fewer takeoffs and landings.

- Choose an airline with a good safety and on-time record.

- Try to make your stopovers in airports with a high security standard and good security screening.

- Try to fly wide-body planes. Hijackers tend to avoid these as they are loaded with too many passengers.

- Most travelers prefer an aisle seat. Choose a window or center seat. This will keep you away from hijackers and any action that may be happening in the aisle.

At the Airport

To diminish the risks of turning from an innocent bystander to the victim of a terrorist attack or other criminal threats, there are a number of things that you should remember when checking into an airport.

- In the event of a disturbance of any kind, go in the opposite direction. DO NOT GET INVOLVED!

- Plan to check in early for your flight to avoid long lines at the ticket counter.

- Go directly to the gate or secure zone after checking your luggage. (Secure Zone - Area between security/immigration and the departure gate.) Avoid waiting rooms and shopping areas outside the secure areas.

- Stay away from glass walled areas and airport coffee shops, which are open to the concourse or public waiting areas.

- From the time you pack your luggage until you check it with the carrier at the airport, maintain positive control of all items, both hand-carried and checked.

- At many airports, security personnel, following Federal Aviation Administration (FAA) protocol, will ask you questions about control of your luggage. Know what items you are carrying and be able to describe any/all electrical items.

- When going through the pre-board screening process, cooperate with security personnel. Remember, they are there to help ensure your travel is safe.

- When arriving at or departing from an airport, try not to exchange items between bags while waiting in line for security screening or immigration/customs processing. Complete all packing before entering such areas.

- If a conflict should arise while undergoing the screening process, cooperate. Obtain the names of the screeners involved. Then, discuss the matter with a supervisor from the appropriate air carrier.

- Remember X-ray will not damage film, videos or computer equipment. Many times such items can be cleared using X-ray, which avoids handling by the screener.

- Consider being transported to/from the airport by a hotel vehicle. Generally the cost is not prohibitive, and arrangements can be made in advance by your travel agent.

- Declare all currency and negotiable instruments as required by law.

- NEVER leave your luggage or briefcase unattended, even while checking in or in the secure zone. In some countries, the police or security forces assume that an unattended bag is a bomb, and your luggage could be forcefully opened or even destroyed.

- Always be aware of where you are in relation to where you are going. If an incident occurs, you need to know how to avoid it and get out of the area or to your boarding area.

- Dress casually when traveling, as this will keep any undue attention from you. Once aboard the flight, remove your shoes for better circulation. Walk around the flight cabin to keep your blood circulating and swelling down.

- Avoid last-minute dashes to the airport.

- Eat moderately, avoid alcoholic beverages and drink plenty of water as this will help to avoid dehydration.

- If possible, in the days before you leave, make an effort to adjust your sleep patterns.

- Sleep as much as possible during the flight.

- Carry airsickness medication with you. Even the best traveler sometimes experiences airsickness.

- Avoid a demanding schedule upon arrival. Give yourself a chance to adjust to your surroundings.

Selecting a Secure Hotel

- Many U.S. corporations have hotels abroad owned by local businessmen and staffed by local workers but managed by first-class U.S. hoteliers. You can usually expect levels of safety and security consistent with U.S. standards.

- Ask the corporate travel agent for a list of recommended hotels.

- Check with the regional security officer at the U.S. Embassy for a list of hotels used by officials visiting the area.

Making Reservations

- Make your own reservations when doing so is practical and consistent with company policies. The fewer people involved in your travel and lodging arrangements, the better.

- If traveling abroad, especially in politically sensitive areas, consider making reservations using your employer's street address, without identifying the company, and using your personal credit card. Again, the less known about your travel itinerary, and whom you represent, the better.

- If arriving after 6 p.m., ensure that reservations are guaranteed.

- Request information about parking arrangements if you plan on renting an automobile.

- Be aware that credit card information has been compromised in the past. Always audit monthly credit card statements to ensure that unauthorized use has not been made of your account.

- Join the frequent traveler programs available through many lodging companies. These programs enable upgrades to executive or concierge floors where available. Be sure to advise the person taking reservations that you are a member and request an upgrade.

Arriving at or Departing From the Hotel

- The most vulnerable part of your journey is any travel between the point of departure or arrival and your hotel. Do not linger or wander unnecessarily in the hotel's parking lot or indoor garage or in public space around the hotel. Be on the alert for suspicious persons and behavior. Watch for distractions that are intentionally staged to set up a pickpocket, luggage theft or purse snatch.

- Stay with your luggage until it is brought into the lobby, or placed into the taxi or limo.

- Consider using the bellman. When your luggage is in the "care, custody and control" of the hotel, the hotel is liable for your property. Protect claim checks. They are your evidence!

- Keep in mind, though, that there are limits of liability created by states and countries to protect hoteliers. Personal travel documents, laptops, jewelry, and other valuables and sensitive documents exceeding $1,000 in value should be hand carried and personally protected.

- If you arrive by auto, park as close to a hotel access point as possible, and park in a lighted area. Remove all property from the car interior and place it in the trunk. Avoid leaving valuables or personal documents in the glove compartment. Before leaving the security of the vehicle, take note any suspicious persons or behavior.

- If using valet service, leave only the ignition key, and take trunk, house or office keys with you. Often, valets are not employees of the hotel and work for contract firms.

- Parking garages are difficult to secure. Avoid dimly lit garages that are not patrolled and do not have security telephones or intercoms.

- Female travelers should consider asking for an escort to their vehicles whether parked in the lot or garage.

Registration

- In some countries, your passport may be temporarily held by the hotel for review by the police or other authorities. Obtain its return at the earliest possible time.

- Be aware of persons in the hotel lobby who may have unusual interest in your arrival.

- If carrying your luggage, keep it within view or touch. One recommendation is to position luggage against your leg during registration while placing a briefcase or a purse on the desk or counter in front of you.

- Ground floor rooms that open to a pool or beach area via sliding glass doors or windows are considered particularly vulnerable. Depending upon the situation, area, and security coverage, exercise a higher level of security if assigned a first-floor room.

- Female travelers should request rooms away from elevator landings and stairwells. This will help prevent your being caught by surprise by persons exiting the elevator with you or hiding in the stairwell.

- Always accept a bellman's assistance upon check-in. Allow the bellman to open the room, turn lights on, and check the room to ensure that it is vacant and ready for your stay. Before dismissing the bellman, always inspect the door lock, locks on sliding glass doors, optical viewer, privacy latch or chain, guest room safes, dead bolt lock on interconnecting suite door, and telephone. If a discrepancy is found, request a room change.

- Ask where the nearest fire stairwell is located. Make a mental note on which direction you must turn and approximately how many steps there are to the closest fire stairwell. In the event of a fire, there is frequently dense smoke and no lighting.

- Also observe where the nearest house telephone is located in case of an emergency. Determine whether the telephone is configured in such a manner that anyone can dial a guest room directly, or whether the phone is connected to the switchboard. Most security-conscious hotels require a caller to identify whom they are attempting to telephone rather than providing a room number.

- Note how hotel staff is uniformed and identified. Many "pretext" crimes occur by persons misrepresenting themselves as hotel employees on house telephones to gain access to guest rooms. Avoid permitting a person into the guest room unless you have confirmed that the person is authorized to enter. This can be verified by using the optical viewer and by calling the front desk.

In Your Hotel

- "All hotel rooms abroad are bugged for audio and visual surveillance." This statement, of course, is NOT TRUE, but that is the premise under which you must operate to maintain an adequate level of security awareness while conducting business abroad. Many hotel rooms overseas *are* under surveillance. In countries where intelligence services are very active, if you are a business person working for an American company of interest to the government or a government-sponsored competitor, everything that you do in that hotel room may be recorded and analyzed for possible vulnerabilities or for any useful information.

With that basic premise established, the following security tips will minimize potential risks:

- **Hotel Room Key**

    Keep it with you at all times. The two most common ways thieves and others determine if a person is in their hotel room is to look at the hotel room mail slot or keyboard or call the room on the house phone. If you do not answer the phone, that is one sign to thieves. But a much clearer signal is the sight of your room key in the mail slot, a visual sign that the coast is clear for a thief or anyone else who might be interested in searching your room and luggage.

- **Upon Arrival**

    Invest in a good map of the city. Mark significant points on the map such as your hotel, embassies and police stations. Study the map and make a mental note of alternative routes to your hotel or local office should your map become lost or stolen. Be aware of your surroundings. Look up and down the street before exiting a building. Learn how to place a telephone call and how to use the coin telephones. Make sure you always have extra coins for the telephone.

    Avoid jogging or walking in cities you are not familiar with. If you must jog, be aware of the traffic patterns when crossing public streets. (Joggers have been seriously injured by failing to understand local traffic conditions.)

- **Valuables**

    Valuables should be left at home. The rule of thumb is, if you neither want nor can afford to lose them, DO NOT TAKE THEM! If, however, you must carry valuables, the best way to protect them is to secure them in your local offices. If that is not possible, the next best course of action is to seal any valuables by double enveloping, initialing across seams and taping all edges and seams before depositing them in the hotel's safe deposit box or safe.

- **Luggage**

  Keep your luggage locked whenever you are out of the room. This measure will not stop the professional thief or intelligence agent, but it will keep the curious maid honest.

- **Passport**

  Keep your passport with you at all times. The only time that you should relinquish it is –

  1. To the hotel if required by law when registering.

  2. If you are required to identify yourself to local authorities for any reason.

  At night, lock your passport and your other valuables in your luggage. This eliminates any mysterious disappearance while you are asleep or in the shower.

  Use a portable or improvised burglar alarm while asleep. Two ashtrays and a water glass are quite effective as an alarm when placed on the floor in front of the entry door into your room. Place a water glass in one ashtray and put the second ashtray on top of the glass. If a straight chair is available, place it next to the door and put the ashtray/water glass alarm on the edge of the chair where it will fall with enough racket to wake you.

- *Guest Room as a "Safe Haven"*

  Hotels are required to provide reasonable care to ensure that guests have a safe and secure stay—but hotels are not required to guarantee guest security. Only you are responsible for your personal security and property. So:

  - While in the room, keep the door closed and engage the dead bolt and privacy latch or chain. A limited number of hotel emergency keys can override the dead bolt locks. To ensure privacy, use the latch or chain!

  - Hoteliers provide guest room "safes" for the convenience of guests. These containers, however, are not as durable as bank safes and can be breached.

Furthermore, the Housekeepers Liability Laws provide that if guest property is not in the "care, custody and control of the hotel," the hotel is not liable. Guests should always place money or valuables in the safe deposit box at the front desk of the hotel.

- When leaving the guest room, ensure that the door properly closes and is secured. Make a mental note of how your property was left. Avoid leaving valuables in plain view or in an unorganized manner. A number of hotel employees enter the room each day to clean, repair and restock the room. Although most hotel employees are honest and hardworking, a few succumb to the temptation of cash or jewelry left unprotected.

- If you determine that an item is missing, conduct a thorough search prior to reporting the incident to hotel security. Do not expect to receive a copy of the security report, as it is an internal document. The incident should be reported to the local police, the regional security and consular officers at the U.S. Embassy, and your insurance carrier. Hotel security can provide a letter verifying that you reported property missing.

- Prior to traveling, copy all credit cards, passport, air tickets and other documents to facilitate reporting loss and replacing them. While traveling abroad, secure these documents in the room safe deposit box and carry copies of your passport and visa.

- Request housekeeping make up your room while you are at breakfast, rather than leave a "Please Service This Room" sign on the doorknob. This sign is a signal to criminals that the room is unoccupied.

- If you are required to use parking stickers in your auto, be sure that they do not indicate your name or room number.

Around the Hotel

Most first-class international hotels spend a considerable sum to ensure your safety and security. Fire safety equipment, closed-circuit televisions (CCTVs) and security patrols are often part of the hotel's security plan. Regardless of the level of security provided by the hotel, you need to become familiar with certain aspects of the hotel's security profile. This will take on increased significance if you are forced to stay at the only hotel at a particular location.

Vary the time and route by which you leave and return to the hotel. Be alert for persons watching your movements.

- Note whether hotel security locks up certain access points after dark. Plan to use the main entrance upon return to the property.

- Speak with the bellman, concierge and front desk staff regarding safe areas around the city in which to jog, dine or sightsee. Ask about local customs and which taxi companies to use or avoid.

- Do not take valuables to the spa or workout room. Note if there are house phones available in the event of a confrontation or emergency.

- Be cautious when entering restrooms in the hotel. On occasion, unauthorized persons use these facilities to deal drugs or engage in prostitution or theft. Female travelers should be alert to placing purses on hangers on the inside of the lavatory doors or on the floor in stalls as these are two frequent locations for grab-and-run thefts.

- Criminals often use areas around public telephones to stage pickpocket activity or theft. Keep briefcases and purses in view or "in touch" while using phones. Caution is urged to safeguard telephone credit card numbers. Criminals wait for callers to announce credit card numbers on public phones and then sell the numbers for unauthorized use.

- Purse snatchers and briefcase thieves are known to work hotel bars and restaurants, waiting for unknowing guests to drape these items on chairs or under tables only to discover them missing as they are departing. Keep items in view or "in touch." Be alert to scams involving an unknown person spilling a drink or food on your clothing. An accomplice may be preparing to steal your wallet, briefcase or purse.

- The pool or beach area is a fertile area for thieves to take advantage of guests enjoying recreation. Leave valuables in the hotel. Safeguard your room key and camera. Sign for food and beverages on your room bill rather than carry cash.

- Prostitutes take advantage of travelers around the world through various ploys, use of "knock-out" drugs, and theft from the victim's room. Avoid engaging persons whom you do not know and refrain from inviting them to your guest room.

In the Workplace

- The workplace, your home away from home: here you are safe and secure. It's the one place where you no longer have to worry about what you do or say. WRONG! You can be just as vulnerable here as anywhere else in the country you are visiting. You probably are safer, but you should still take some precautions.

- Safeguard all sensitive or proprietary papers and documents. Do not leave them lying around in the office or on top of a desk.

- Guard your conversations. Do not allow unauthorized personnel to eavesdrop on discussions pertaining to proprietary information, personnel issues or management planning or problems. In many countries, employees are debriefed by the local intelligence or security services in an effort to learn as much as possible about activities of American companies and their personnel.

- Be careful of all communications. Be aware that the monitoring of telephone calls, telegraph communications and international mail is common in some countries.

Traveling by Train

In many countries, railroads continue to offer a safe, reliable and comfortable means of travel between major metropolitan areas. Other countries, however, operate antiquated rail systems that are often over-crowded and seldom run on time. As a general rule, the more socially and economically advanced a country is, the more modern and reliable its rail service will be. Frequently, rail travel provides a more economical method of travel than other modes of transportation. Often it is the only available transportation to smaller cities and towns. However, rail travel can present some security risks to the traveler, just like other means of travel.

Railroads are "soft" targets for several types of criminal or terrorist attacks. They operate over open ground and are easily accessible to the public. The tracks on which the trains operate are in the open for most of the distance they cover. This easy accessibility provides an inviting target for bombings and other forms of sabotage.

The railroad terminals and stations are like self-contained cities, open to the public for 24 hours a day. They provide a fertile ground for pickpockets, purse-snatchers, baggage thieves, bombers and other criminals to operate.

Trains themselves offer similar opportunities to criminals and terrorists. A train is like a hotel on wheels, offering temporary accommodations, such as restaurants, sleeping space, bars and lounges. All of these can be, and often are, subject to criminal activities, including robbery, thievery, bombing and even, albeit rarely, hostage taking.

Security Risks

Generally, railroad terminals and trains are easy targets for the following types of attacks:

- Theft of unattended baggage on board trains and in rail terminals

- Thefts from sleeping compartments

- Robberies and burglaries

- Bombing and other forms of sabotage to railroad tracks, terminals and trains

    Just as air travel calls for planning and preparation to lessen the risks of unfortunate experiences, rail travel also requires certain preventive measures to lessen the likelihood of the traveler becoming a victim. Some simple yet effective precautions can help make a rail trip a comfortable and convenient means of moving between or within many countries of the world.

Some Precautionary Measures

Prior to departure:

- It should be noted many cities have more than one railroad station. Travelers should confirm which station their train will depart from in advance. Make sure that you use the right one.

- Make reservations in advance to avoid long lines at rail station ticket counters. This is where pickpockets, baggage thieves and purse-snatchers like to operate. Your hotel concierge can assist in making reservations and picking up your ticket.

- Travel light and always keep your luggage under your control. In the time it takes to set down your luggage to check a timetable, a baggage thief can make off with it.

- Watch your tickets. Keep them in an inside pocket or purse to lessen the chance that they can be stolen.

- Do not discard your train ticket until you've completed your trip and have left the arrival area. In some countries you will be required to show your ticket at the station exit. If you do not have it, you may be required to purchase another one. Hold on to your ticket, whether or not a conductor checks it.

- Make certain that you board the right car and that it is going to your intended destination.

- Find out in advance whether your car will have to be switched to another train en route, when and where this will occur, and the name of the stop just prior to the switching point. Prepare accordingly.

- If you have to transfer to another train to reach your destination, determine this in advance and know where you will make the transfer, the time of transfer, the train number and departure time of your connecting train, and the track number if possible.

- Learn how to tell whether you are in the correct car and whether it goes to your destination. Name boards on the side of the car will tell you this.

For example, a name board that appears like this:

VENEZIA

Bologna - Firenze

ROMA

This shows that the car begins in Venice, stops in Bologna and Florence, and ends in Rome.

Next to the steps leading into many train cars you should see the numeral "1" or "2," or both. The "1" indicates first class. The "2" indicates second class.

Make certain you know how to spell and pronounce the name of your destination city so you recognize it when announced.

Be alert to train splitting. This occurs when part of the train is split off and attached to another train while the remainder of the original train then continues on its way. Check with the ticket agent or on-board conductor to determine whether this applies to your itinerary.

Try not to schedule a late night or early morning arrival. You might find yourself stranded at a rail station with no public transportation.

Arrange to be met at your arrival point whenever possible.

On Board the Train

- If possible, check unneeded luggage into the baggage car.

- Keep your unchecked luggage with you at all times. If you must leave your seat, either take your luggage with you, or secure it to your seat or the baggage rack with a strong cable-lock.

- Try to get a window seat. This provides a quick means of escape in the event of an accident.

- Have necessary international documents, including your passport, handy and ready for inspection by immigration officials at each border crossing.

- Always keep your camera and other valuables with you at all times.

- If you have a private compartment, keep the door locked and identify anyone wishing to gain access. Know the names of your porters and ask them to identify themselves whenever entering your compartment.

- When in your compartment, be aware that some train thieves will spray chemicals inside to render the occupant unconscious, then enter and steal valuables. A locked door will at least keep them out.

- If you become suspicious of anyone, or someone bothers you, notify the conductor or other train personnel.

- If you must leave the train temporarily at a stop other than your destination, make certain that you are not left behind.

- An understanding of military time (the so-called 24-hour clock) will make it easier for you to understand the train schedule.

- Make certain you have currency from each of the countries through which you will be traveling. In some lesser-developed countries (and on some trains) it may be advisable to carry your own food and water.

Upon Arrival

- Make certain that you depart from the train at the correct location.

- Use only authorized taxis for transportation to your hotel or other destination.

- Be alert to criminals such as pickpockets, baggage thieves and/or unauthorized taxi drivers/guides.

- If you do not have a hotel reservation, go to the in-station hotel services and reservations desk for help in obtaining a hotel room.

Driving Abroad

Before you drive, use the acronym POWER to remember important times:

P   **Petrol/Fuel:** half tank or more at all times

O   **Oil:** no noticeable leaks, level is good

W   **Water:** no noticeable leaks, level is good

E   **Electronics:** lights, dash, GPS, radio, cell phone

R   **Rubber/Tires:** good tread, spare good, hoses

- Obtain an International Drivers Permit (IDP). This can be purchased through your AAA Club. Have your passport photos and a completed application. There will be a fee involved. Carry both your IDP and your state driver's license with you at all times.

- Some countries have a minimum and maximum driving age. Check the laws before you drive in any country.

- Always "buckle up." Some countries have penalties for violations.

- If you rent a car, always purchase the liability insurance. If you do not, this could lead to financial disaster.

- As many countries have different driving rules, obtain a copy of them before you begin driving in that country.

- If the drivers in the country you are visiting drive on the opposite side of the road than in the U.S., practice driving in a less populated area before attempting to drive in the heavy traffic.

- Be vigilant when driving through the countryside. Many countries require you to honk your horn before going around a sharp corner or to flash your lights before passing.

- Find out before you start your journey which lane has the right of way in a traffic circle.

- Always know the route you will be traveling. Have a copy of a good road map, and chart your course before beginning.

- Do not pick up hitchhikers or strangers.

- When entering your vehicle, be aware of your surroundings.

Personal Conduct Overseas

A hostile or even friendly intelligence organization is always on the lookout for sources vulnerable to coercion, addictions, greed or emotional manipulation. To eliminate, or at least diminish, the possibility of doing something inadvertent that would bring your activities to the special attention of one of these agencies, here are some things to remember:

- DO NOT do anything which might be misconstrued or reflect poorly on your personal judgment, professional demeanor, or embarrassing to you and/or your company.

- DO NOT gossip about character flaws, financial problems, emotional relationships or marital difficulties of anyone working for the company, including you. This type of information is eagerly sought after by those who would like to exploit you or another employee.

- DO NOT carry, use or purchase any narcotics, marijuana, or other abused drugs. Some countries have very stringent laws covering the import or use of medications and other substances. If you are using a prescribed medication that contains any narcotic substance or other medication that is subject to abuse, such as amphetamines or tranquilizers, carry a copy of the doctor's prescription for all medications and check your local restrictions and requirements prior to departure. Some countries may require additional documentation/certification from your doctor.

- DO NOT let a friendly ambiance and alcohol override your good sense and capacity when it comes to social drinking. In some countries, heavy drinking in the form of toasting is quite common. Very few Westerners can keep up with a local national when it comes to drinking the national brew. An intoxicated or hung over business negotiator could, if not careful, prove to be very embarrassing and expensive to the company. In these situations, prudence is essential.

- DO NOT engage in "black market" activities, such as the illegal exchange of currency, or the purchase of religious icons or other local antiquities.

- DO NOT accept or deliver letters, packages or anything else from anyone unknown to you. You have no way of knowing what you are carrying, and it could result in your being arrested for illegally exporting a prohibited item.

- DO NOT engage in any type of political or religious activity, or carry any political or religious tracts or brochures, or publications likely to be offensive in the host country, such as pornography or mercenary/weapons.

- DO NOT photograph anything that appears to be associated with the military or internal security of the country, including airports, ports, or restricted areas such as military installations. If in doubt, err on the side of caution.

- DO NOT purchase items that are illegal to import such as endangered species or agricultural products.

I've Been Arrested! — What Do I Do Now?

Foreign police and intelligence agencies detain persons for a myriad of reasons or for no other reason than suspicion or curiosity. The best advice is to exercise good judgment and be professional in your demeanor. If you are detained or arrested for any reason, here are some points to remember:

- DO ask to contact the nearest embassy or consulate representing your country. As a citizen of another country, you have this right. But that does not mean that your hosts will allow you to exercise that right. If you are refused or just ignored, continue to make the request periodically until they accede and let you contact your embassy or consulate.

- DO stay calm, maintain your dignity and do not do anything to provoke the arresting officer(s).

- DO NOT admit anything or volunteer any information.

- DO NOT sign anything. Often, part of the detention procedure is to ask or tell the detainee to sign a written report. Decline politely until such time as the document is examined by an attorney or an embassy/consulate representative.

- DO NOT accept anyone on face value. When the representative from the embassy or consulate arrives, request some identification before discussing your situation.

- DO NOT fall for the ruse of helping the ones who are detaining you in return for your release. They can be very imaginative in their proposals on how you can be of assistance to them. Do not sell yourself out by agreeing to anything. If they will not take no for an answer, do not make a firm commitment or sign anything. Tell them that you will think it over and let them know. Once out of their hands, contact the affiliate or your embassy for protection and assistance to get out of the country.

Help for Americans Overseas

The Bureau of Consular Affairs, Overseas Citizens Services, is committed to assisting American citizens who become victims of crime while traveling, working, or residing abroad. Government officials, known as consuls or consular officers, are posted at embassies and consulates in nearly 250 cities throughout the world. They are responsible for assisting U.S. citizens who may be traveling, working, or residing abroad. In addition, in approximately 50 cities where a significant number of Americans reside or visit and there is no U.S. embassy or consulate, consular agents provide emergency assistance to U.S. citizens. Consuls, consular agents, and local employees work with their counterparts in the Bureau of Consular Affairs Overseas Citizens Services Office in Washington, D.C., to provide emergency and non-emergency services to Americans abroad.

Before You Go

Enroll in the **S**mart **T**raveler **E**nrollment **P**rogram (STEP). The STEP Program is a free service of the Bureau of Consular Affairs that allows U.S. citizens and nationals traveling abroad to enroll their trip with the nearest U.S. Embassy or Consulate. In other words, the U.S. Embassy or Consulate in the country you are visiting will know that you are "in country" and can assist travelers in need. The STEP program helps travelers by:

•   Providing important information from the Embassy about safety conditions in your destination country. This helps you make informed decisions about your travel plans.

•   Helping the U.S. Embassy contact you in an emergency, whether natural disaster, civil unrest, or family emergency.

•   Helping family and friends get in touch with you in an emergency.

The US Department of State also developed a free App for your smart phone or tablet that allows you to participate in the STEP program, receive alerts/warnings and research specific country information all from your device.

How to Contact

Consular duty personnel are available for emergency assistance 24 hours a day, seven days a week, at embassies, consulates, and consular agencies overseas and in Washington, D.C. To contact the Office of Overseas Citizens Services in the U.S., call 1-888-407-4747 (during business hours) or 202-647-5225 (after hours). Outside the U.S., 1-202-501-4444. Contact information for U.S. embassies, consulates, and consular agencies overseas is on the Internet.

If You Are the Victim of a Crime Overseas

- Contact the nearest U.S. embassy, consulate, or consular agency for assistance.

- Contact local police to report the incident and obtain immediate help with safety concerns. Request a copy of the police report.

- Consular personnel can provide assistance to crime victims. When a U.S. citizen becomes the victim of a crime overseas, he or she may suffer physical, emotional or financial injuries. Additionally, the emotional impact of the crime may be intensified because the victim is in unfamiliar surroundings. The victim may not be near sources of comfort and support, fluent in the local language, or knowledgeable about local laws and customs.

- Consuls, consular agents, and local employees at overseas posts are familiar with local government agencies and resources in the country where they work. They can help American crime victims with issues such as:

  - Replacing a stolen passport

  - Contacting family, friends, or employers

  - Obtaining appropriate medical care

  - Addressing emergency needs that arise as a result of the crime

  - Obtaining general information about the local criminal justice process and information about your case

- Obtaining information about local resources to assist victims, including foreign crime victim compensation programs

- Obtaining information about U.S. crime victim assistance and compensation programs

- Obtaining a list of local attorneys who speak English

- Consular officials cannot, however, investigate crimes, provide legal advice or represent you in court, serve as official interpreters or translators, or pay legal, medical, or other fees for you.

Individual Reactions to Crime Victimization

How individuals react to being the victim of a crime varies based on individual factors, such as how the victim handles stress, the nature and duration of the crime, the physical safety of the victim, and the number and type of support systems available. Reactions to a crime may be immediate or delayed. The physical, emotional, or cognitive symptoms a victim may experience could include nausea, headaches, fatigue, hyperventilation, or sleeping problems. Some victims report feelings of anxiety or fear, hypervigilance, guilt, anger, or isolation. Some experience difficulty making decisions, short-term memory problems, difficulty concentrating, or recurring memories of the crime.

It is important to realize that these are normal feelings, behaviors and reactions to an abnormal event. One of the first things to pay attention to is your need to feel safer. Addressing safety concerns and receiving emotional support can help. For most victims the reactions described above diminish with time. If these reactions persist and are disrupting your life or getting worse after three or four weeks, you should consider seeking professional assistance.

Resources and Information for Crime Victims

Victim Assistance: If you are the victim of a crime while overseas you may benefit from specialized resources for crime victims available in the U.S. Throughout the United States, thousands of local crime victim assistance programs offer help to victims of violent crime. Most will also help residents of their community who have been the victim of a crime in another country. These include rape crisis counseling programs, shelter and counseling programs for battered women, support groups and bereavement counseling for family members of homicide victims, diagnostic and treatment programs for child abuse victims, assistance for victims of drunk driving crashes, and others.

Victim Compensation: All states operate crime victim compensation programs and nearly half of them offer benefits to their residents who are victims of violent crime overseas. These state compensation programs provide financial assistance to eligible victims for reimbursement of expenses such as medical treatment, counseling, funeral costs, lost income or loss of support, and others. Generally, victim compensation programs require the victim to report the crime to law enforcement. They usually request a copy of the police report.

"There are no foreign lands.
It is the traveler only who is foreign."
—Robert Louis Stevenson

Chapter 7 Review
Practice Assignment – Travel Preparation and Planning

How Well Did You Prepare?

This chapter has explored the ways you should plan and prepare before you begin your trip. It also discusses the details of travel —both the ins and outs of hotels and transportation. Finally, you learned about what to do if you are unfortunate enough to be mistakenly put in jail in a foreign country and what resources are available for victims of crimes overseas.

Now, let's put some of that knowledge to work with a practice scenario.

Practical Example

- Semi-permissive environment (area with some government control).

- Traveling for business and encountering a series of unfortunate events.

You've finished up a meeting in Shanghai and your business associate recommends you enjoy the countryside in China. He suggests you take a train to your next meeting in Beijing. So, you purchase a ticket for a soft sleeper, which includes a comfy four-berth area with two sofa beds and a table. There is a locking door, which you like a lot. You are a little confused going through the security check, but everything seems in order and you board the train. You aren't sure about how to check luggage, so you decide to haul your two suitcases along with you. You settle in and start to work on your laptop. But, then several individuals come into the compartment. You didn't realize that you were sharing the space. The people seem okay. You gesture and make friends.

Everything goes along well until the conductor comes in to check tickets. Where did you place your ticket? You can't find it. You try to explain, but the language barrier is a problem. The conductor is not happy. There is an interim stop. You are taken off the train and are still trying to explain what has happened. You offer to pay, but by this time, the train has departed. You look around. During the confusion, you were distracted, and your briefcase is missing. Now you are panicked. Your briefcase contained your passport and most of your funds. You alert an attendant, but he shrugs, not understanding. You start to get really upset. This upsets the attendant, who feels threatened. Suddenly, a uniformed officer is on the scene. You feel relieved, but this feeling only lasts a second because you are being arrested.

Study Guide Questions

What should you do next to mitigate your arrest?

What could you have done to prevent this situation from happening in the first place?

Study Guide Answers

What should you do next to mitigate your arrest?

First, ask to contact the nearest embassy or consulate representing your country. As a citizen of another country, you have this right. But that does not mean that your host will allow you to exercise that right. If you are refused or just ignored, continue to make the request periodically until they accede and let you contact your embassy or consulate.

Remain stay calm, maintain your dignity, and do not do anything to provoke the arresting officer. Do not admit anything or volunteer any information.

The officer in charge asks you to sign something. You can't read it since it is written in Chinese. You decline, knowing that part of the detention procedure is to ask or tell the detainee to sign a written report. You decline politely and determine you will wait until the document can be examined by an attorney or an embassy/consulate representative.

Someone finally comes in saying they are from the U.S. Embassy. You ask for identification, which is provided. You proceed to explain that your passport was stolen along with your briefcase.

What could you have done to prevent this situation from happening in the first place?

Unfortunately, you didn't retain your ticket for the train, and this led to your being inattentive—and then your briefcase was stolen. Inattention was the cause of all this misery. You should have been more attentive. But you did everything right once you were taken into custody. You kept your cool. You asked for a representative of your government, and you made sure to check the representative's documentation. The embassy representative was able to explain your situation, and you were soon able to put this unfortunate event behind you.

NOTES:

References Chapter 7

American Automobile Association www.aaa.com.

Carjacking: Don't be a Victim, Overseas Security Advisory Council, Department of State, OSAC Publication 2005.

Centers for Disease Control and Prevention, Division of Global Migration and Quarantine, National Center for Preparedness, Detection, and Control of Infectious Diseases, Atlanta GA, 2009.

Burton, Fred. Stewart, Scott. Threats, Situational Awareness and Perspective, Terrorism Intelligence Report, August 2007.

Business Travel Abroad, Department of State, Overseas Security Council, Diplomatic Publications, Released 1994.

Counterterrorism, The National Counterterrorism Center, Counterterrorism Calendar, September 2008.

Glossary of Terms

"The world is a book and those who do not travel read only one page."

—St. Augustine

Agencies – Intelligence and law enforcement agencies are government agencies devoted to collecting information related to host government security and defense. These agencies may collect information on travelers, including proprietary corporate information.

Alert Mode – Alert Mode is one of the stages in the Modes of Awareness cycle. It is the constant observation of the environment and scanning for potential threats. A person should be in Alert Mode at all times. Time in Alert Mode may last days, weeks, or months. Transition to from Alert to Pre-Crisis Mode is triggered when potential threats are recognized. To prevent stalled decisions and actions, invisible thresholds are set, and the OODA loop is used to help make decisions.

Body language - Non-verbal physical movements and expressions communicate intentional or non-intentional thoughts and emotions. A simple yet powerful body language signal is when a person crosses his or her arms. Other than indicating that a person is physically cold, this typically indicates an unconscious barrier has been raised.

COMSEC - A process by which a group or individual can deny adversaries information about intentions by identifying, controlling, and protecting evidence of the planning and execution of travel.

Crisis Mode – Crisis Mode is one of the Modes of Awareness stages. It is the tactical action against the threat to dominate, elude, or escape the threat. This is not the time for decision-making. That process should have been completed in Pre-Crisis Mode. Crisis Mode is triggered by the breach of the invisible threshold. Crisis Mode may last seconds or minutes. Transitioning back to Pre-Crisis Mode should occur sooner rather than later. Increased exposure to the threat may decrease survivability. Threat domination, elusion, or escape trigger the transition back to Pre-Crisis Mode.

Cultural Awareness (CA) – This is the assessment and understanding of a specific geographic location's culture, including cultural-specific aspects such as social protocol, etiquette, mannerisms, gestures, and other Personal Awareness traits. Cultural Awareness coupled with Personal Awareness can help decrease Third Party Awareness and help you navigate through possible threats undetected.

Daisy chain – This type of surveillance can be used instead of a floating box to decrease possible compromise of the operation. A daisy chain is a passive, static multimember linear surveillance where individual surveillants are staged along the known route of a target person. The surveillants are typically ahead of the target person, observing and reporting the target's arrival and departure at specific locations along the target's route.

Demeanor (actions) – The image you convey is defined as your physical actions, which include gestures, manners, language, handshake, walk, and speech and other things the general public can observe. Chapter 4 is dedicated to country-specific culture projection and demeanor traits for you to use during travel.

Environmental threats – Environmental threats include natural disasters and threats like hurricanes, tsunamis, winter storms, volcano eruptions, and mudslides. You need to learn what hazards are common in the area you will be visiting and how to handle challenges should they arise.

First-line gear (difficult to change) – As it relates to projection, this is your birthday suit. You want to identify any characteristics that are culturally offensive, make you stand out in a crowd, or make you a threat.

Floating box – Once the target moves from location to location, then this type of surveillance may be used. A floating box is defined as a multimember mobile surveillance box that discreetly surrounds the target person during foot or mobile movement. Each member rotates in and out of position to maintain constant observation. This tactic is very difficult for a team to perfect and risk of compromise is high.

Health threats – Health threats consist of, but are not limited to, viruses, bacteria, chemicals, and other harmful substance spread human-to-human, airborne-to-human, water or food-to-human, and vector-to-human. Other types of health threats include air pollution and animal or insect bites. It's important to know what health threats are common in the area you plan to visit and prepare before your trip.

Intrusion detection – Discreet techniques and tactics that can be used to determine surveillance status.

Non-permissive environment (No U.S. policy exists) – A non-permissive environment, sometimes called a denied area, is an area where there is little or no government. Control is induced through hostile actions of non-government forces. Support of the United States or its citizens is minimal. Country example: Syria.

OODA loop – This four-step process helps with decision-making. The steps are Observation, Orientation, Decision, and Action.

Permissive environment (U.S. policy exists) – A permissive environment is an area under complete control by the government. The government is supported 100 percent by its citizens. The most important part: the host government and its citizens support the United States. Utopia, if you will, where everyone lives in harmony. Not sure a permissive environment truly exists. Canada maybe?

Personal Awareness (PA) – The image and demeanor you project to blend in within a specific culture, reduce threat vulnerabilities, and reduce Third Party Awareness. Personal Awareness ensures an individual assesses and manages specific character traits that separate him or her from the intended culture of interest. Personal Awareness is also the ability to recognize and identify your physical characteristics and the actions that personify your individual projection and demeanor.

Physical surveillance – When an individual or group of individuals physically follow, observe or track a target's every movement.

Pre-Crisis Mode – One of the Modes of Awareness stages. Pre-Crisis Mode is the constant observation of the identified potential threats. Time in Pre-Crisis Mode may last hours or days. Pre-Crisis Mode is triggered by the identification of a potential threat. This mode allows a person to determine courses of action and designates an invisible threshold that activates Crisis Mode. All decisions made in this mode prepare you to transition to Crisis Mode for action. When the threat breaches the invisible threshold, Crisis Mode is initiated. To prevent stalled decisions and actions, invisible thresholds are set, and the OODA loop is used to make decisions.

Projection (appearance) – This is your physical appearance, what the general public can observe, and includes clothing, jewelry, technology, grooming standards, gender, race and accessories.

Protocol – International rules and social behavior, such as body language and communication, in accordance with a specific culture. Protocol includes meetings, greetings, manners and other actions within a culture.

Raids/robbery threats – An organized assault conducted by criminals or terrorists. By definition a criminal is a person guilty of a crime or crimes. Criminals commit theft, rape, murder and everything in between. The most significant raids to highlight are carjacking, kidnappings and hostage situations.

Second-line gear (easy to change) – As it relates to Projection, encompasses anything that touches your skin. Second-line gear includes things like hats, sunglasses, shirts, pants, underwear, socks, gloves, necklaces, bracelets, watches and rings. These items make up a large part of the traits that define a person and are used to separate them from others.

Semi-permissive environment (U.S. policy may exist) – A semi-permissive environment has a government that yields questionable control. The citizens may or may not support the government. The government and citizens may or may not support the United States. Corruption is usually the wolf for these countries. Country example: Philippines. Most of the world is semi-permissive.

Setting the box – Most surveillance teams "pick up" a target from a static location like home or work. To "set the box" is defined as multimember static surveillance covering all four sides of a structure. Each position assigned is in direct relation to possible exit and entrance points used by the target person. One of the team members will observe the target person departing or entering the structure and report a positive identification, location, dress, and activity to the rest of the team.

Situational Awareness (SA) – This is a conscious and constant focus on the environment to detect, validate, and confirm threats. Detection is triggered by both instinct and observation.

Surveillance – This assessment of vulnerabilities in an attempt to determine any information available from any source about you or your activities, such as lifestyle or behavior that can be used against you (pattern of life).

Technical surveillance – This type of monitoring consists of following, observing and tracking of a target with electronic equipment.

Technological threats – Technological threats include audio collection devices, video collection devices, tracking devices, cell phone exploitation, and laptop exploitation used to collect information illegally. It's important to understand what each threat poses and what defenses and actions can be taken.

TEDD – This acronym stands for Time, Environment, Distance and Demeanor. If you see someone repeatedly over time, in different environments and over distance, or one who displays poor demeanor, then you can assume you're under surveillance.

Terrorism – A person or group using unlawful acts of violence to influence, coerce, or strike fear into people for ideological, political, or religious gains. Currently, there is not an internationally agreed definition of terrorism. You should research and learn about terrorist facts, groups, and tactics related to the area you plan to visit.

Third-line gear (remains through change) – As it relates to Projection, this covers anything that touches your clothes. Third-line gear includes items like jackets, shoes, belts, man bags, purses, backpacks, wallets, passports, mobile phone and laptops. These are items that people use for long periods of time (longevity items) or have in limited quantities when traveling.

THREAT – This acronym is a risk assessment tool used to define technical, health, raid, environmental, agency, and terror threats in a specific geographically location. Using this acronym will help you assess and research potential threats, which will sensitize your senses, prep your Situational and Personal Awareness, and decrease your vulnerabilities.

Third Party Awareness (3PA) – This is the general public's perception of you and your actions. In a nutshell, when you feel like everyone is staring at you, they probably are. Third Party Awareness includes citizens, law enforcement, criminals, and terrorist residing in the host country. To reduce Third Party Awareness, you need to blend into the environment by using Personal Awareness (culturally driven projection and demeanor management) and Situational Awareness skill sets.

The Total Awareness System (TA) – This holistic risk assessment system reduces threat vulnerabilities through Situational, Personal, Cultural, and Third Party Awareness. The Total Awareness system includes pre-deployment threat assessments, cultural assessments to blend in, heightened awareness, and identifying and escaping threats.

"Not all those who wander are lost."
—J.R.R. Tolkien

CPSIA information can be obtained
at www.ICGtesting.com
Printed in the USA
BVHW042023041019
560242BV00002B/186/P

9 781598 589672